Texas Rhapsody

*

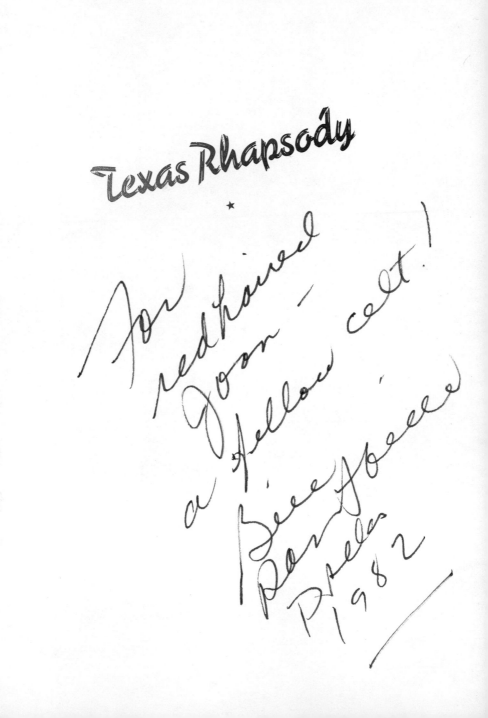

For
redhaired
Joan —
a fellow
Celt!

Best
Regards
1982

Texas Rhapsody

Bill Porterfield

MEMORIES OF A NATIVE SON

HOLT, RINEHART AND WINSTON
NEW YORK

Published by Holt, Rinehart and Winston,
383 Madison Avenue, New York, New York 10017.

Published simultaneously in Canada
by Holt, Rinehart and Winston of Canada, Limited.

Library of Congress Cataloging in Publication Data

Porterfield, Bill.
Texas rhapsody.

1. Texas—Social life and customs. 2. Porterfield,
Bill. 3. Texas—Biography. 4. Journalists—Texas—
Biography. I. Title.
F391.2.P63   976.4′009′92 [B]   80-28611

ISBN: 0-03-059294-1
FIRST EDITION
Designer: Susan Mitchell
Printed in the United States of America
1 3 5 7 9 10 8 6 4 2

The author wishes to thank the Dallas Times Herald, D Magazine, and Vision Magazine
for permission to reprint stories originally published by them.

The following stories originally appeared in the Dallas Times Herald: "Lupe and Moon's
People"; "In the Old Man's Footsteps"; "Where Have You Gone, Joe DiMaggio? A Nation
Waits"; "Aunt Arbie, Our First Liberated Woman"; "Daddy, Mother, and Uncle Charlie";
"Looking for a Lost Love at the State Fair"; "Uncle Eddie: The Long and Short of It"; "A
Bright Kite and a Prayer for Ma"; "Deep within Her Heart Lies a Memory"; "Ma's Valiant
Battle"; "The Wakefield House"; "Juneteenth with Sassmouth"; "The East Texas Icarus";

"In Archer City Even Movie Fame Is Fleeting"; "The Ugly Mexican"; "Coming of Age in Just Another Little Town"; "A Cracker Jack Secret"; "Colleen, Coach, and the Class of 1950"; "Cecilia and the Confessions of a Male Chauvinist" (originally published as "Cecilia and the Confessions of a Chauvinist"); "Mance and Elnora's River Bottom Love"; "The Dear Men in Her Life"; "The Rose of Sharon"; "Turn About Is Fair Play"; "How Bois d'Arc Sam Took the Cowpokes"; "The Midnight Dancer"; "The Hungry Hitchhiker"; "The Honey Lady"; "The Widow and Her Dream House"; "A Mexican Standoff at the Crystal Ball Nite Club"; "The Priest Who Didn't Belong"; "Ernie Rucks: Vegetable Peddler"; "The Man Who Counted His Money Too Much"; "The Edification of James"; "Death and Dominoes in the Park"; "The Taskmaster at Samuell Grand"; "A City Dweller Panning Fool's Gold"; "Cub Reporter Days with Dan Rather"; "Hildy Harris, Front-Pager"; "At the Tavern with Preston Jones"; "J. Frank Dobie: Bring Him Back Alive"; "The Reporter Who Exposed Billie Sol"; "Skeeter Hagler's Big Day at the Paper"; "Adieu, Preston, a Man Can Die But Once"; "June Bugs and an Old Bird of Paradise"; "Young Nanette, Old Willie, and Billie"; "Across the Red River This Son Will Go"; "A Little Time and a Few Kind Words."

The following stories originally appeared in D Magazine: "Of Salty Girls, Inchworms, and God's Face" (originally published as "The Tramp"); "The Last Willful Testament of Emil Schnittker."

The following story originally appeared in Vision Magazine: "The Blessing of the Witch Bitch" (originally published as "The Blessing of La Bruja Perra").

Grateful acknowledgement is made for permission to quote from the following works:
On A Slow Boat To China by Frank Loesser, © 1948 Frank Music Corp., Renewed 1976 Frank Music Corp. Letters To A Young Poet by Rainer Maria Rilke (translated by M. D. Herter Norton), by permission of W. W. Norton & Company, Inc., copyright 1934 by W. W. Norton & Company, Inc., copyright renewed 1962 by M. D. Herter Norton, revised edition copyright 1954 by W. W. Norton & Company, Inc. Norwood, by Charles Portis, c/o International Creative Management © 1966 by Charles Portis. My Wild Irish Rose, words and music by Chauncey Olcott, from A Romance In Athlone, 1899, MDCCCXCVIII by M. Witmark & Sons. This Is My Beloved by Walter Benton, copyright 1943 by Alfred A. Knopf, Inc., renewed 1971 by Walter Benton. The Collected Poems of Wallace Stevens, © 1942 by Wallace Stevens, reprinted by permission Alfred A. Knopf, Inc.

The story "Where Have You Gone, Joe DiMaggio? A Nation Waits" has appeared in newspapers in the United States under the auspices of United Feature Syndicate, Inc.

For Bobby Lee Porterfield—
hermano, compadre, amigo, paisano

★

ACKNOWLEDGMENTS

★

I would have experienced these people, but probably wouldn't have written about them if Ken Johnson and Will Jarrett at the *Dallas Times Herald* hadn't said, "Come sit down beside us and tell some good stories." Writers have always needed patrons, so I'm beholden to Ken and Will.

Carol Edgar helped me see the little book, shuffled through the deck picking out aces and queens and kings like an Amarillo Slim. Being musical, she found the title for me. And, contrary to what my old man thinks, I didn't type the manuscript that went to the literary agent and ultimately the publisher. Lynnda Bass did that, and more. Typists are not supposed to comprehend as they fly through the pages, but Lynnda did, setting me straight when something didn't fit. Still, what arrived at Holt, Rinehart and Winston was not the genuine article, and it took editor Tom Wallace and his assistant, Jackie Cantor, to make the final sense of it. Tom was a low-calorie Perkins to my Wolfeish literary bulimia.

Finally, I'm in debt to my agents, Aaron Priest and Molly Friedrich. Aaron has been both pushy and patient with me for a long time. Back in January of 1978, he wrote: "Where are you? I have not heard or received anything from you.

You were going to send me some material, a story, a novel, an old shoe, something. Not one comma has arrived. If I was not so poor, I would call you. I talked to A.C. and he tells me you have woman troubles. If so, you have my deepest sympathies. I had hoped it was nothing serious like jail or disease. At any rate, let me hear something." It took me three years, but this is what Aaron heard.

B.P.

rhap'so·dy *n.*, [pl. -DIES]. [Fr. *r(h)apsodie*, L. *rhapsodia*, Gr. *rhapsoidia*, *rhapsoidos*, one who strings songs together, reciter of epic poetry, *rhaptein*, to stitch together (IE. *werp-*, to twist, wind, whence WRAP, RAVEL) + *oide*, song (see ODE)] 1. *a*) in ancient Greece, a part of an epic poem suitable for a single uninterrupted recitation *b*) a similar modern literary work 2. any ecstatic or extravagantly enthusiastic utterance in speech or writing 3. great delight; ecstasy 4. [obs.] a miscellany 5. *Music* an instrumental composition of free, irregular form, suggesting improvisation.

— Webster's New World Dictionary
of the American Language

CONTENTS

★

Part Six ★ COLLEAGUES

EPILOGUE

Part One

★

KITH AND KIN

★

The horrible truth instantly flashed across me—the horse tracks I had been following were my own; since the preceding morning I had been riding in a circle.

—Charles Sealsfield,
Adventures in Texas, 1893

LUPE AND MOON'S PEOPLE

★

That summer I lived with Uncle Ardmore and Aunt Moon in Cotulla, we did most of our grocery buying at Sleepy's in Mexican Town, where staples were cheap. It was also convenient. We lived around the corner. We had never lived right among Mexicans before, but the rent shack was all we could find that we could afford. The oil rig Uncle Ardmore was to work on hadn't spudded in yet and we were busted, anxious for a payday.

Uncle Ardmore never said much about the Mexicans one way or the other. Maybe it was because Aunt Moon herself was part Mexican; at least she was Indian, a squaw from the Ysleta tribe of El Paso. She made a big deal about being an Indian who easily passed for white, and she pretended not to understand or speak Spanish. Well, actually she secretly spoke Tex-Mex, the border patois that Mexican nationals called *pocho*. I always thought it sad that Anglos down there never learned their neighbors' language. Daddy and Uncle Ardmore made the Mexicans come to them, so to speak, on their own terms. Today, when I hear that little roughneck Bill Clements pronounce the Mexican president's name as Poor-Tillo, emphasizing both *l*s, I cringe. A governor of a state where one of every six citizens is of Mex-

ican extraction ought to know better. Oh, well, Bill is off the
same rig floor as Daddy and Uncle Ardmore.

On Sundays we would go to Jesus's Café for Indian food,
which we loved with a gluttony. Uncle Ardmore would
leave the ordering to Moon. She would look over her long
sable nose at the menu and speak out of the redneck side of
her mouth, affecting a nasal twang while pretending to mis-
pronounce the dishes.

"Well, let's see," she would say, "the kid wants beef tacos
and a little waw-camo-lee salad. Ardmore, do you want the
Spanish dinner?" He'd nod and she would order two dinners
and four bottles of Mexican beer. The menu clearly read
"Mexican Dinner" and not "Spanish Dinner," but this was
Moon's way of not offending the waitress. It was okay to be
"Spanish" in Texas then, but nobody wanted to be "Mexi-
can," not even the Mexicans themselves.

Lupe, the dark little woman who lived next door and took
care of the parish priest, made a point of insisting she was
Spanish, when it was as clear as the pigment in her skin that
she was closer to being pure Indian than anything else. She
had a face like an Aztec warrior, strong and noble as folk-
lore. I look back on Lupe now with a tinge of sadness. She
never knew who she was in a larger sense. She had no cul-
tural memory.

I would have been proud to have her and Moon's blood,
but of course I knew the magnificence of her lost heritage
because Father Daspit had told it to me. Poor, ignorant
Lupe did not know it. It seemed that none of her people
knew it, or if they did they let on that they didn't. I was just
a kid, as Moon constantly reminded me.

Father Daspit and I were an odd pair, as out of place in
the desert as the asparagus and orchids he tried to grow
around the rectory. I was an anemic child of the Reforma-

tion, a pint-sized freckle-neck drifter raised on fundamentalist predestination and damnation, and he was an Old World scholar in the primitive New World, a large and wilting Vincentian priest whose superiors had forgotten they had left him out in the chaparral. But we shared a passion for the people of the Southwest.

They are all dead and gone now—Father Daspit, Lupe, Moon, and Uncle Ardmore—as dry and dusty in their graves as the heap that was Cotulla. I am hundreds of miles and years away from them, stuck up here in the mercantile north country, hounded by the clock and materialism. But once in a while I dream now as I dreamt then on those opiate afternoons in the shirking shade of the mesquite beside Father Daspit's rectory.

Lupe and the priest are on their knees in his sad garden grunting and gasping and scratching at the hot, hostile earth. The town is dreadfully dusty and subdued, almost dolorous in the heat, and I hear no sounds but the heaving and clawing of the gardeners and the bleating of a goat bound for the barbecue pit and the hum of the highline wires on the road to Laredo. A lizard crawls from under a stone and blinks in the sun. It blinks away a thousand years and I am naked, stained by earth and sky, a golden boy in a land of sunshine, silence, and adobe. I know the cactus and the coyote and the lizard and the snake and the spider, and live with them and the chill of the night in harmony. But I do not know the Spanish conquistadores or the Anglo colonists, for they have not yet come. The latter will become my father's people. But I do not know this because in my dream I am Lupe and Moon's people.

IN THE OLD MAN'S
FOOTSTEPS

★

My father, being a roughneck and a driller, wanted me to become a geologist. He saw me following his footsteps in the oil field, but wearing soft, expensive loafers instead of steel-toed boots. He saw me as an educated man on the rig floor, one who wrestled with seismic graphs and symbols instead of pig iron and mud. He wanted me to have what he had not had, and yet he wanted me to do it within the context of his own occupation. This way I would mature into a true extension of him. It would make him proud, because it would mean that his work was more than just drawing wages, that it was indeed a saga that sons found irresistible.

We would come to speak the same language, seek the same goals, share the same fraternity. Daddy never said it this way. In fact, he never said much about anything. But I knew.

I was also enthralled with the idea.

My first memories of my father are powerful ones. Now I realize he was the archetypal male, that what he did was what men had done since the dawn of the race. We could have lived in a cave instead of an oil-field shack.

Workaday winter mornings were always cold. The house was like an icebox. But Daddy would get up before sunrise and light the fires. Then he would crawl back in bed with Mother until the rooms warmed up. Sometimes, in my half-sleep, I could hear them talking. Daddy's voice was so deep in the morning it idled like a great engine set in neutral. By five they were up and in the kitchen, eating breakfast and preparing lunches.

We kids went off to school with sandwiches in paper sacks. Daddy went off to the rig carrying a tin lunchbox. We kids ate meat spreads and peanut butter and jelly, always on white bread. Daddy ate what we called "Dagwoods," after the old comic-strip character. I've seen Mother stack a fried egg, a slice of rat cheese, a hunk of smoked beef, a slab of onion, a wedge of tomato—soaked in Tabasco—between two pieces of bread and hear Daddy complain that she was serving him tearoom sandwiches.

Daddy ate sausage and meat loaf and chicken-fried steak, always on white bread. He had grown up on an Oklahoma farm on dark, heavy, homemade bread. So store-bought white bread was a refinement to him. When Daddy met a man who was doing well and flashing money, he always said, "That fella is living the white-bread-and-red-beer life."

It seemed to me that the oil patch Daddy went off to was a magical place, much like a place from a fairy tale. He wore a lot of iron and tin, like a knight of old, and what he did every day was to try to slay, or at least harness and control and ride, the metal monster that shook and screamed in the sky as it pawed into the earth.

Roughnecks were often getting hurt, sometimes killed. Daddy himself had had a lot of injuries and close calls. He always came home bloodied with oil, his khakis caked with mud and grease. He smelled like a volcano, like the center of the earth. His big hands had guy wires for fingers and Texas crude under the nails. His face was a bed of thorns.

In the long tropical summers, when we lived back deep in the sand and ticks, waiting for Daddy to come home was the high point of those drowsy, monotonous days. It was even better than waiting for the mail.

The house was like an oven, and the little floor fans Mother set out only circulated hot air, their drone adding to the torpor that engulfed us. The idea for us kids was to find comfort, some cool, wet place, and doze and dream at child's play until noon, when Mother would call us for iced tea and sandwiches. The mail wouldn't come until early in the afternoon, so back to our burrows we would go until time to walk to the mailbox out at the crossroads.

Finding those special places, and keeping them a secret from Mother, became a game. If she found us, she would flush us out and make us help with the chores. Even in the heat, Ma was Mrs. Perpetual Motion. When she was not at the stove stirring up something, she was on her knees scrubbing the linoleum, or at the roller washing machine and clothesline, or bent over the ironing board pressing khakis and jeans. She even ironed the bed sheets and Pa's drawers. The only time I saw her relax was Sunday afternoons, when she would clip commonplace verses from the big-city paper and paste them in her book of memories. She smelled of soap and starch and scorched cotton, and there was always bluing on her chubby fingertips. But it made her proud. She liked to say you could eat off her floors they were so clean, that Daddy wore the only starched underwear on the drilling rig.

We couldn't hide in the cornfield. The earth was so hot, the stalks so dry and yellow and razorlike, the husks so full of spiders and bugs, that it was alien territory.

We couldn't hide in the woods. It was the pits—steamy, rutty ravine land, scarred by erosion, soured by stagnant swamp, crawling with snakes and alligators and gar that literally fed on one another to stay alive. Even the vines and vegetation fought for life, entwining and squeezing one another in a mad, upward spiral for air and sunlight. Lungs and gills and pores struggled to breathe in the humidity.

But we were safe and cool under the wooden water tower beside the windmill. Daddy had wrapped the substructure beams in canvas, had plugged a couple of holes in the bottom of the tank so that water would drip down on the crocks of milk and butter and cheese that Mother kept there. We would lift the linen off the jars, dip dirty fingers into the sweet cream, and skim it up and suck it into our parched mouths. Whenever Mother caught us, she would get a switch and try to whip us. We would run around and around the water tower, naked little savages, giggling at the poor lady who for the life of her couldn't catch us. She would see how absurd it was too, and start to laugh. She never laid a hand or the slightest switch on us. Daddy would beat the bloody dickens out of us, but Ma didn't, wouldn't if she could have cornered us. The windmill turned and squeaked in the wind, the pump sang, the water trough filled, and she would run with us as we raced the cows to drink from it and skinny dip.

Banned from the milk house, we were buoyant in the boughs of the chinaberry tree. It grew in a clearing at the edge of a slimy creek, ever green in all that wilt, and from its crown of camouflage we would throw berries at the great, horned spiders that had fenced the woods with their webs.

It seemed to us that everything out there was mean and hostile, that all manner of things—mineral, vegetable, animal—either pricked or pounced or was poisonous. Even the lizards wore spikes. Daddy said the only soft things in that whole country were featherbeds and the underbellies of horny toads and women. During the day all those creatures lay on rocks and at the edge of their holes, sleeping wth slit eyes, the better to see you coming. But at night they came alive and crawled and thrashed about, hunting, killing, moaning and groaning and crying out mating calls, and I would lie on my bed with my head in the window and listen to that swarming din and feel a tide of shivers ebb and flow the length of my spine. My only comfort was the deep rumble of Daddy's snoring.

But the nights were cool.
And there were great tins of iced tea at noon.
And the mail came in the afternoon.
And Daddy came home after that.
The mail truck was too far away for us to hear it.
But we knew.

A little alarm clock went off in us. We would gather on the porch and wait for Mother. She would come out in her bonnet, and, at our urging, remove her shoes. The challenge, the delicious pain of it, was to scamper through the blistering sand of the road all the way to the mailbox and back. It was maybe a mile each way, and the only relief to and fro was an occasional patch of shade from a tree.

That poor woman. The soles of our feet were tough as shoeleather, hers were as soft and tender as the underbellies Pa dreamed of. How she stood it I'll never know. It was like walking on fire. If you had to stand still, you stood on one foot and then the other. But it was worth it because of the sweet reward a bit of shade offered. We walked through heaven and hell to get the mail.

When there was nothing in the box, the road back home

was a long one. But that was rarely the case. If there wasn't a letter, there was always something, a circular, a catalogue. The junkiest thing was reason to rejoice. It meant that as far out in the sand as we were, as hot and miserable as the live-long summer was, that someone, somewhere, was thoughtful enough to send us something, even if it was an advertisement or even a bill. We would hotfoot it home, but not to read it. That was the old man's prerogative, his and only his, no matter if it was a letter to Mother from one of her sisters.

Mother would take it, no matter how significant or insignificant it was to our lives, and leave it on the smoking tray Daddy kept beside his easy chair. When he came stomping in from the rig, deep-voiced and heavy-booted, smelling of oil and mud and sweat and tobacco, and now and then of whiskey, before he did anything, before he even took off his tin hat, he would stride up to Mother, who by this time was back at the stove, pinch her on the butt, and say, "Jenny, any mail today?"

"What came is where it always is," she would say.

The ritual began. He would settle in his chair and light his pipe and open the mail while the kids unlaced and removed his boots. Then we would settle around and he would read it, first to himself and then aloud.

"Hummm. The Sir Walter Raleigh Smoking Tobacco Club wants me to join up for an initiation fee of a dollar fifty. For that I get a free tin of tobacco and a certificate of membership suitable for framing. And let's see. A good deal on future premiums."

"Why, how nice, Tice," Mother said. "That's awful thoughty of them. Why don't you go ahead and do it? It would look nice hanging on the wall over your chair."

"Well," he said, obviously pleased, "I'll have to think about it."

He would remove his armor and soak in a hot tub, soaping himself with the harsh grit of Lava. That night, slick as a whistle, his belly full of supper, he would sit by the radio and relax. Now he smelled of a dash of aftershave, a shot of whiskey, tobacco.

It was a manful, mysterious world I would enter only in apprenticeship. By the time I was in college I worked the oil patch only for pay, for tuition money. I had my heart set on being a journalist.

Daddy was flabbergasted.

"You're studying what?" he asked.

"Journalism," I said. "I want to be a reporter. You know, work for newspapers."

We only got a Sunday paper, and all he had ever read was the comics.

He never said another word about it.

That was twenty-nine years ago.

In all that time he has never come to see me in the cities where I have lived. I must go to him.

I have written something like six million words in my work, and he has read damn few of them.

I have covered murders and manhunts, and talked to men about to sit in the electric chair. I have reported from the eye of hurricanes. I was with Meredith and King and Carmichael when they marched through Mississippi. I have been roughed up by rednecks because I was "a nigger-loving newsman." I have been beaten by rioting blacks because I was "a honky newsman." I have sat down with whores and princesses. I have talked to astronauts and assassins. I have supped with presidents and sipped with peons. I have entered worlds my old man cannot imagine.

But he thinks I type for a living.

"Patterson, I want you to meet my son, Billy."

"Hidy, Mr. Patterson."

"Where you live, Billy?"

"Dallas."

"Boy, what do you do?"

I look at Daddy. He hates anyone putting on airs. "I type for a living."

"Oh," Patterson says, and changes the subject.

The old man ain't too proud.

But what can you do? You try to raise them right, but you never know how they'll turn out.

Take my daughter.

Erin never reads my stuff either. She's been saying for the last couple of years that she wants to go into business and make a lot of money. She's tired of being broke, of living with a mother who is a professor and now a father who is a hack. I tease her about becoming a vice-president for McDonald's International. She worked at one of the hamburger stands for a while, and was fascinated by the precision and profit of mass production.

But the other day she came home from SMU and said she thought she would like to become a reporter.

I tried not to show it, but I was touched. I tried to be offhand about it.

"Are you sure you want to follow in your old man's footsteps?"

She looked at me in surprise.

"Oh," she said, "I hadn't thought of that. I guess you are, or were, a reporter. But no, Dad, you're right, I don't want to be like you."

"Well, where did you get the idea?"

"From watching TV," she said. "I love Lou Grant. Now that's the kind of reporter I'd like to be."

WHERE HAVE YOU GONE, JOE DIMAGGIO? A NATION WAITS

★

It is a part of the American rite of spring, and to a man my age, it is almost as rejuvenating as a rerun of an old Marilyn Monroe movie. Get me a beer and a hot dog and a seat behind first or third and I am a boy again, breathing in rhythm to every pitch, my heart leaping at the crack of a bat. It is better to be at the ball park, of course, but that's beginning to be a luxury. Most of the time television has to do, just the way radio used to. Ah, time and technology change, but the game remains the same. And now the season is upon us. The Rangers are in Detroit for the opener against the Tigers. I wish them well, but I must confess that in my heart of hearts the hometown team for me is still the Yankees. That may sound funny, since the closest to New York I ever lived was Detroit. But don't you see, it was the radio that took me to Yankee Stadium almost every day of the season when I was a kid. In fact, I saw but one big-league game while growing up, and it turned out to be one of the great moments in baseball, although at the time I didn't appreciate that fact. To tell the truth I was sorely disappointed.

It was the ominous summer of '41. Daddy had turned forty that spring and was grouchy about it. War was raging in Europe and Asia, and everyone said there was no way we were going to stay out of it. Politics was no better at home. That hillbilly singer, Pappy O'Daniel, had just whipped a young New Deal Congressman, Lyndon Johnson, for the Senate, and besides that Daddy was drilling a dry hole on the Armstrong Ranch down in Kenedy County.

The only bright spot was Joe DiMaggio of the New York Yankees. About the middle of May, Joltin' Joe began a batting streak that lasted into July. It caught the fancy of the whole country, and diverted us, for a few months, from the specter of war. And down in Norias, Texas, near the Mexican border, we were just as enthralled as any fan from Manhattan. Of course we couldn't see the Yankee Clipper—the nearest major-league club was in St. Louis, eight hundred miles away—and there was no television. We hung by the radio, and my old man was the most faithful of all. He never missed a Yankee game.

On July 1, 1941—I think it was a Sunday because Mother was out in the yard wringing a fryer's neck for supper—Daddy went off his rocker. He jumped out of his radio chair and ran outside, whooping and hollering and clearing barbed-wire fences like a high hurdler.

"What's got into the old fool?" Mother asked me, a chicken head in her fat little hand.

"DiMaggio just homered against the Red Sox," I said. "That breaks the record. Old Wee Willie Keller's record, you know, of hitting safely in forty-four consecutive games! Well, old Joe just did it, Mother, he just did it, and that's what's got hold of Daddy."

When Daddy settled down, he made a major, prewar decision. For once in our lifetimes, before the Nazis and Japs and gas rationing got us and the rest of the country down, the Porterfields were going to see a major-league baseball game.

"And what I want to do," Daddy said, "is to get up there and see DiMaggio before his streak runs out."

The old man had a Terraplane Hudson that he never drove over forty miles an hour, which meant we had to make tracks. Daddy called in another toolpusher to straw-boss the drilling, and on Sunday, July 13, we loaded up the Hudson and headed for Cleveland, Ohio, fifteen hundred miles away, where, in four days, DiMaggio and the Yankees would be playing the Indians.

The day we left we got off to a late start, because Daddy had to listen to the game on the radio. Joe kept his string alive in a double-header against the Chicago White Sox, so it was dark before we drove off.

We didn't have a car radio, and we didn't have a portable, so we used gas-station attendants along the way to keep us posted on Joe's progress. DiMaggio's heroics, heightened by broadcasting, exploded across the land like Fourth of July pinwheels, and along our route the excitement was kinetic. It was the only time in our family history that Daddy was willing to make Mother's rest stops every forty miles. We ate cheese and crackers and drank Cokes and spent the night in tourist courts that advertised a radio in each room.

On Monday, as we bore down on the Louisiana-Arkansas border, the Yanks lost to the White Sox, but DiMaggio beat out a bounder to third and kept it alive at fifty-four games.

Tuesday, between Memphis and Louisville, we heard that Joe had doubled and singled against Chicago.

On Wednesday, stalled in Columbus with a boiling radia-tor, we listened in a service station as Joe stayed alive with a double and two singles against Cleveland. That made it fifty-six.

We roared into Cleveland the next day, in plenty of time. It was a night game, and I had never seen so many people in my life. There were 67,000—at that time a major-league attendance record—and Mother said most of them were standing in line ahead of us. She and my sister got tired of waiting and chickened out. They begged off and went to a movie. It was a soppy film about a home for girls in Fort Worth, starring Greer Garson and Walter Pidgeon. *Blossoms in the Dust*, I think it was. Daddy was profoundly disgusted with the women in our family.

We men, Daddy and my brother and I, made it in.

All night long, the great DiMaggio never got one out of the infield. On Joe's last swing, when he hit into a double play, Daddy turned to me with a sour look on his Texas face and said, "Them Eye-talians will do it ever' time. Fold in the stretch!"

Things weren't as good in real life as they seemed to be on the radio. We headed home to winter and war and FDR's death and Harry Truman's inauguration, which people in sixteen cities saw on television! Already things were changing.

We even got to see old Joe DiMaggio play a time or two on TV. But he was never as good as he had been on radio.

AUNT ARBIE, OUR FIRST
LIBERATED WOMAN

★

Old Man Potter was the neighborhood grump. Nothing pleased him. He was out of sorts with everything—the war abroad, the patriotism and sacrifice on the home front. He hated Truman and Churchill and Hitler in the same breath. But the person he hated most was my Aunt Arbie. I think it was because she wore britches and could cuss a blue streak. She also blew her whistle at him a lot. It was because he wouldn't turn out his lights during blackouts. Arbie was our Civil Defense block captain, our air raid warden.

One evening when Arbie was parading around in her tin hat and uniform, almost wishing an honest-to-goodness real air raid would come so she could show her stuff, Mr. Potter said to me with disgust: "Look at your aunt! I'm a silly old fool but I've learned a thing or two. I used to think that the only thing that would save man from destroying himself was for women to take over the world. I thought they were different, superior somehow. Now, knowing old Arbie there, I'm not so sure. I'm afraid they can make just about as big a mess of things as we do. Rats! It'll just be more of the same. Now that they've started to dress and talk like us, what's to keep them from acting like us?"

Well, in a sense he was right. If ever there was a woman who wanted to be one of the boys, it was my aunt. I don't mean to say there was anything butch about Arbie. On the contrary, even then, in her forties, she could turn old Earl around with one of her dark, direct gazes. She was part Choctaw, and Uncle Earl used to tell us he had to chase her down barefoot in the woods of Oklahoma to woo her. He was six-feet-one and barrel-chested, a suntanned boss of oil-field men, and she was five-feet-four and fuming, a slip of a woman who was obviously frustrated in the traditional role society had made for her sex.

Arbie was the first woman in our family—except for the old maids—to say flat out that, no, she did not want children. And she held to it. She was the only woman in our family to smoke a cigarette and cuss in public. My paternal granny dipped snuff while cursing the evils of smoking tobacco, and my mother was careful to delete her colorful expletives when company was around, but Arbie was out front. She even drank beer in bottles while sitting in her car at drive-ins. *In broad daylight.* That's how bold she was.

She was the first to learn to drive a car, the only female in the family who could change a flat tire. Earl was a big hunter, but Arbie was a better shot and she took better care of her gear. She could cast a rod and reel as accurately as Zeus hurled thunderbolts, and of course her heroine was the great Babe Didrickson. When the Babe married and changed her name to Zaharias, Arbie got a little antsy. She was afraid the Babe would bloom forth with child instead of staying free and easy to chase a golf ball for thirty-six holes a day. Arbie was funny about kids. She didn't want to fool with having her own but she was great with someone else's. She practically adopted my brother and me and kept us almost every summer. When we became Cub Scouts, Aunt

Arbie went down to Sears and bought a uniform too and became a den mother.

She was hooked on uniforms and had an outfit for every occasion. That's why I always suspected that Aunt Arbie helped start the war. Just before the Japs bombed Pearl Harbor, rumors were rife that we were going to war, and I figured that every night Arbie went to bed praying for it to commence. Our men got kind of down on her. Heck, here Daddy and Uncle Earl were fortyish and almost draftable— certainly they could have gotten into the army if they had wanted—but they chose, as they put it, to stay home and produce the fuel for our fighting boys. Arbie, on the other hand, was fit to be tied. At breakfast, she would tell us how in her dreams the night before she had led the invasion into North Africa, or had stood with MacArthur at Bataan. It was all we could do to keep her from joining the WAVES or the WACS. She settled for being a Civilian Defense worker, and made of it an exciting, soldierly career all through the war. She patrolled our block in a resplendent red, white, and blue uniform with sergeant's stripes and a helmet, blowing the whistle on people like Old Man Potter who kept their lights on during blackout drills. Every day she searched the skies with a telescope, looking for enemy planes. None came, of course. But we did have some natural disasters—a couple of hurricanes down on the coast, a defense-plant explosion or two—that allowed Arbie to do more than walk up and down the block. She became a firefighter and drove one of those big red jobs to the rescue. When it was all over over there, when the boys came home and Arbie had to hang up her uniform, she did it with not a little sadness. Later, however, it became a source of pride, her part in the war effort, and Uncle Earl bragged on her a lot.

Later, as an idealistic kid in college, my pride in my aunt turned to something darker. I began to see her through Old Man Potter's eyes. It disturbed me that Arbie's liberation had to take the form of male destructiveness. Madame Curie in the laboratory, Babe on the golf course, Mabel in a Mack truck were one thing, but had a woman gained something because she had mastered the deadly gadgetry of our times and marched around gullible to group-think, chanting slogans and saluting? She could shoot and kill ducks, Arbie used to say, as good as a man and better than Earl, and if she had gotten into the war as a soldier I imagine she would have given Audie Murphy a run for his medals. Well you can see that, in my downy-cheeked boyishness, I had put women on a pedestal. I've taken them off it now.

I'm not as bitter and pessimistic about their moving up into lockstep with the men as Mr. Potter was. As Arbie put it as she smoked and drank and cussed, "I'll pick my own poison. Fair is fair." In my more optimistic moments I agree with the German poet, Rainer Maria Rilke, who in 1904 forecast the coming of women's liberation in America. He said, "Girls and women in their new, their own unfolding, will but in passing be imitators of masculine vices and virtues and repeaters of masculine professions. After the uncertainty of such transitions, it will become apparent that women only went through the whole range and variety of these (often ridiculous) disguises in order to clean their own characteristic nature of the distorting influences of the other sex."

Well, I sure hope so. Course we men needn't get in a flap about it. Uncle Earl said, with an eye to Arbie, women were going to do what they wanted to whether we liked it or not, and that we'd just as well get used to it. Hell, he said, he was having a hard time just keeping up with Arbie.

DADDY, MOTHER,
AND UNCLE CHARLIE

★

Daddy felt fortunate to have come across Uncle Charlie after all those years. He wasn't kin. We called every older man we liked "uncle," and Charlie was likeable. He had been Pa's best friend in Saudi Arabia. In fact, Charlie had been the one who had pulled some strings to get my old man on a crew that was bound for the Persian Gulf. They had spent four years over there running rigs and roughnecks for King Saud and his Texas oil producers, making, as Daddy put it, money hand over fist so fast you couldn't count it. Of course most of it ended up in the king's coffers and in the pockets of the big boys, but Daddy and Uncle Charlie got more than enough to satisfy them.

My old man came back with enough of a grubstake to start him a trailer court in Seguin and retire from the oil patch, and Uncle Charlie, well, he spent his on doctors and druggists trying to save his wife from cancer. This we learned later, because the two old drillers had lost touch with one another after they got back to the states. One day Daddy came home whooping and hollering. "Mama," he said, "you can blow me down if I'm lying, but guess who I saw at the pool hall awhile ago?"

She put her hands on her hips. "Well," she declared, "it has to be that big bankroller we been waitin' on to drill the lease in Oklahoma and make us rich."

"Naw, woman, you're silly. I just seen a sight for sore eyes: Uncle Charlie."

"Charlie? Well, I swan! What's he doing here?"

"He's moved here. Can you beat that? We both end up in the same place after all these years."

"Lordy, lordy," Mother said, "I'll have to call Colleen and invite them over."

"Ye cain't," the old man said. "Colleen died some years ago. Charlie's alone now, kids all grown up and gone."

"Poor Charlie."

"Yeah, I felt sorry for him. He ain't the same man. You know he used to be such a banty rooster. Now he's old and feelin' poorly. I think he said he was eighty-one, six years older'n me."

"Well, we'll have to look after him."

"Mama, you're exactly right. That's why he's coming for supper tonight."

They were old men now. Their drilling days were over. But they liked to sit out on the trailer patio beneath the mesquite trees and talk big about the times they had had in the oil patch. They told each other about how they told so-and-so just how the cow ate the cabbage. They relived, in outsized hyperbole, every fistfight and blowout, every honky-tonk high and hangover, casting themselves in every telling as taciturn heroes in the frontier mold, men of few words but men of clean and decisive action. They talked saga and they talked oil technology.

Mother had heard oil talk all her life and she smiled at the stretchers and even the outright lies. Daddy hadn't been so happy in a long time, stranded as he was in a country of conservative farmers and ranchers who'd never been out of the county. So Uncle Charlie was welcome. He was, in his effect on Daddy, both antidotal and anecdotal. And Mother liked him because he was that rarity in the oil patch, a courtly, old-fashioned gentleman who did not seem uncomfortable in the company of women. He had marvelous manners.

Daddy is a man of unswerving habit. You can set your watch by his routine. Every afternoon just before Uncle Charlie came over he would go down to Baenziger's to buy something. Even if the larder was full he'd have to make the trip to complete the day. One evening when he was gone the phone rang in the trailer house and mother picked it up. To her astonishment a man began singing:

> My wild Irish rose,
> The sweetest flower that grows,
> You may search everywhere,
> But none can compare,
> With my wild Irish rose . . .

Mother thought it was a joke, some family friend playing a trick. She laughed and asked, "Who is this?" But whoever it was hung up. And that bothered her. Odd. But she put it out of her mind.

The next afternoon, as soon as Daddy left for Baenziger's, it happened again, just as before.

It continued through the week. It was a damned nuisance. It was not the voice of some kid. It was a man, an old man with a high, shaky voice. It was, she decided, an obscene phone call, obscene in its furtive and suggestive nature. The words themselves and the sentiment were in strange contrast, beautiful and courtly in an old-fashioned way.

She hadn't wanted to tell Daddy, but finally she did. The

next afternoon he stayed home from Baenziger's, and when the call came Mother answered and then handed him the receiver. He listened to the man singing and then quietly hung up and called the police to put a tracer on the call.

Police traced the call to Uncle Charlie.

You could have knocked Mother and Daddy down with a sledgehammer.

They would have never suspected him, not Daddy's old friend, not the Charlie of Charlie and Colleen, not the gentlemanly octogenarian widower Uncle Charlie.

Charlie confessed up to the police, but Daddy didn't let them charge him with anything. Instead he sent word for Uncle Charlie to come by the trailer house, as usual. He did. He drove up and got out and went over and sat down with Daddy on the patio under the mesquite trees and started crying.

"Why did you do it, Charlie?"

"I don't know. I've always loved and respected Jenny. You both have been so good to me. You are my best friend. Something just came over me. I don't know why I did it. I guess I miss Colleen. I'm ashamed. I wish I were dead."

"Well," Daddy said. "A man can do some strange things. But he can right them, too. I'd appreciate it if you'd step in the door there and apologize to Jenny. She's waitin'. That's all we ask."

And that's what Uncle Charlie did, crying all the time and with Mother and Daddy trying to comfort him.

He was too embarrassed to come back around after that. Daddy told him to forget it and come and see them, but Charlie couldn't. It was not long afterward that his land-lady found him dead in bed. He had died in his sleep of a heart attack. Daddy and Mother located his kids and helped bury him.

LOOKING FOR
A LOST LOVE AT THE
STATE FAIR

★

Uncle Eddie rode a bus all the way in from Florida to see the State Fair. He does this every year. I always pick him up at the Continental Trailways station on Jackson and we make a day of it at Fair Park. Along about dark I drop him off at the beer joints on Exposition, where he holds forth until it is time for him to stagger out and catch a cab and make the early morning bus back to Jacksonville.

Uncle Eddie pretends to enjoy the fair, and I guess he does, but the real reason he makes his annual pilgrimage is to look for Jean Furella. You see, Jean is his long-lost love, and Uncle Eddie thinks that someday she will turn up in one of the freak shows along the midway. Now this will take some explaining, but first let me give you a little background about my family and particularly Uncle Eddie.

In the olden days the whole Porterfield clan, as Celtic as demons and druids, was as wee as leprechauns. In fact, in the fancy of family lore our ancestors in medieval Scotland and later Ireland were dwarfs with storied powers both poetic and supernatural. We grew a little larger up through the generations until none of us but Uncle Eddie could be called a midget. In fact, for years he passed himself off as the World's Smallest Perfect Man until he got fat, and then he claimed he was the World's Smallest Perfect Fat Man. Charles Portis must have met him because he wrote beautifully about a man I take to be my uncle in the novel *Norwood*. The hero runs across an "Edmund" in a beer joint in Jacksonville and is struck by him.

"Them are regular little hands you got."

"Of course they are."

"If you were out somewhere without anything around, like a desert, and I was to start walking towards you I would walk right into you because I would think you were further off than what you were."

"I've never heard it put quite that way. Well now it's a matter of scale. I'm not a dwarf, you know."

"Maybe you don't like to talk about it."

"No, it's all right, I'm not the least bit sensitive. I do dislike the way newspapers throw the word around. 'Governor So-and-So is a moral midget.' That annoys me."

As you can see, Uncle Eddie is a charming little gentleman. He usually does himself up in a nice little black suit that has to be custom-made. If he wasn't so small you would forget he is a circus freak and think maybe he is a foreign dignitary or something. But the sad fact of it is that he is a carny man. It is a rough-and-tumble life, one that creates an even greater gulf between a guy like Uncle Eddie and so-called normal people. He hadn't dared let himself yearn for the stability and affection that marriage and children can bring. What woman could love a little weirdo like him?

Well, Jean Furella, that's who. She fell madly in love with

Uncle Eddie. He was crazy about her, too. Indeed, he was deeply flattered that a full-sized woman, one so beautiful and shapely, would find him attractive. But there was one thing wrong. Jean had a beard. It turned Uncle Eddie off. He couldn't bring himself to kiss her. "Off," he said, "off with the beard. Shave and I'll marry you."

Jean Furella was heartbroken and defiant. The beard was her badge, her shining glory, the basis of her career along the bright lights of the midway. She would not shave it off. Instead, she ran off with John Carson the barker and married him. Uncle Eddie never got over it. Later, when he heard that Carson had died, he began his search to find Jean and win her back, no matter how hairy she was.

So last week, as soon as we passed through the gates of Fair Park, Uncle Eddie found out where the freak show was and hurried to it with me in tow. We bought our tickets and stood impatiently inside the tent while a menagerie of grotesques went through their routines. There was everything imaginable except a bearded lady. Percilla the Monkey Girl had a lot of hair on her legs and arms and a few straggles hanging from her chin, but she definitely was not Jean Furella.

"Well," Uncle Eddie sighed, "let's make the best of it and go ahead and enjoy ourselves."

And we did. We ate corny dogs and cotton candy and rode the Hurricane. We drank beer and tapped our feet to Nick Nixon and His Country Soul Music. We paid George Howard a buck apiece to put our signatures into his personality computer. Out came a profile of Uncle Eddie that said: "You prefer slow, steady progress to sporadic success. Indecision in others annoys you. You have an easy-going manner admired by others. You love luxury and extravagance. You keep busy constantly and you can't stand boredom." It seemed to please Uncle Eddie.

It was sad, though, looking at Abraham Lincoln in the wax museum. "They do his face okay," Uncle Eddie said, "but his body is all wrong. It's too short and out of proportion to that great head. You know Lincoln was afflicted with the Marfan syndrome. That's what made him such an elongated freak. It's a bone disease, shows up about the fourth generation in certain families, and this is where your giants come from you see in carnivals and sideshows. Lincoln inherited it from his great-great-grandfather, Mordecai Lincoln II, and I'm betting that it would have killed him if Booth hadn't. Marfan men don't live very long."

We cheered up at Jack Mullane's House of Heraldry booth inside the Centennial Building. Uncle Eddie gave Jack a dollar to find out if the Porterfield family had ever been issued a coat of arms. Jack said it was all on the up-and-up, that if the name had not been registered he would not make up a coat of arms. He would simply return the dollar. Jack picked up a paperback book entitled *What's in a Name: Surnames of America*. No Porterfield there. Then he looked in a larger book called *The Dictionary of British Surnames*. We weren't there either. Uncle Eddie frowned. "I'm afraid," he mumbled, "that there wasn't much to our forebears."

"Oh, don't be discouraged," Jack said. "I've yet to look in the bible of British heraldry. Ah, here 'tis!" He dropped a huge thick tome upon the counter. The dust of ancient glories seemed to rise from it like myrrh. I could hear clans marching and bagpipes. The title page read, "*The General Armory of England, Scotland, Ireland and Wales*, by Sir Edward Burke, C.B., LL.D., Ulster King of Arms." And therein, on page 816, was the Porterfield register. It said, in heraldic code, that we were of the County Renfrew ilk of Scotland, and that our coat of arms had, upon its field of black and red, a stag's head and a hunting horn and a palm branch, and that the motto upon the crest was *Sub pondere sursum*. In difficulty I looked upward.

"That," said Uncle Eddie, "is most appropriate."

He placed an order with Jack for a coat of arms to be made and mounted and mailed to him in Jacksonville. We left the fair and went down to Jimmy's place for a beer. I left him there, a dapper little man braced with brew and the arms of heraldry, holding forth about life and love, and trying to make out with a woman named Mary Sue, who had spent the day parking cars and was too tired to tell him to shut up.

UNCLE EDDIE:
THE LONG AND SHORT
OF IT

★

Uncle Eddie writes from his trailer house in Florida that he is failing and may not live out the year, and that, under the circumstances, he feels justified in urging me to come and help settle his affairs.

His main concern, he said, is that I be briefed on the progress of the study that has occupied him since his retirement, in the hope that I can see to its posthumous publication. His magnum opus, in fact his only opus, is based on his unswerving belief that the small human being is superior, over the long genetic haul, to the large human being.

His claim is that in the beginning nature made man too big for his own good, that nature quickly realized its mistake, and has since been whittling him down to a finer proportion. Uncle Eddie waves off vital statistics that show a general increase in size in almost every generation in America and Europe. A momentary inclination, he says, not amounting to much on the whole scale of human history. *Scale* is one of his favorite words.

I am going to get over to see him, and soon, and expect

to get a story or two out of the trip. At least one facet of his work is certainly timely. He has made a study of the heights of presidential candidates since the birth of the republic, and of how popular notions about the size of men prejudice the outcome of elections and color our history.

Now I am not a midget, but Uncle Eddie taught me early to take advantage of my short stature. For example, he so built up my ego when I was a schoolboy that I was able to make the varsity football team as a halfback. This encouraged me to try out for the team at Del Mar Junior College in Corpus Christi. The head coach, Ox Emerson, took one look at me on the first day of camp and laughed. "Charlie Dollar would make two of you," he snorted, and sent me home. Dollar was a Little All-American, Del Mar's smallest running back. So there I was, living in the music dorm with a bunch of sissies, trying to make the choir, for God's sake. I was pretty down-in-the-mouth, so one weekend Uncle Eddie rode a Continental Trailways bus into Corpus to cheer me up.

We went to a beer joint and had a session.

"Look," he said, "by not making the football team you have saved yourself from the gladiator ring. Don't get down in the pit with the brutes. Go up into the emperor's box with the brains."

"That's easy for you to say," I said. "You have no choice."

"Neither do you," he said. "Emerson isn't an ox for nothing. He won't move, so accept it. Think of it this way. Size and primitiveness go hand in hand. Anthropology supports it and so does religious myth. The Bible says, Genesis 6:4, that 'there were giants in the earth in those days.' And Lord knows literature is full of titans: Polyphemus, Goliath, Gargantua, Rubezahl, Gog and Magog.

"Science concurs. Two of our earliest specimens of man,

the giant from Java—Meganthropus—and the giant from Hong Kong—Gigantopithecus—were bigger than gorillas. In the human evolutionary line, the more primitive the form, the more gigantic the dimensions. Early man was much larger than modern man. And yet who would deny our superiority? Dear boy, remember the wisdom of Didacus Stella, who said that a dwarf standing on the shoulders of a giant may see farther than the giant himself."

Sure, Uncle Eddie admitted, now and then there were reversals: the dwarf who played the house fool, the intelligent giant. But, he insisted, most of the movers and shakers—Socrates, Hannibal, Caesar, Christ, Mohammed, Cortez, Voltaire, Rousseau, Napoleon, Franklin, Einstein—were physically frail types who had used their wits and will and special gifts to prevail. Davids against Goliaths.

Churchill had been a marvelous example. Here was a small, sensitive boy, bullied and beaten at school, who grew up into a short, fat man. He had a chicken chest with no hair on it. His arms were thin and his hands were a woman's. He spoke with a lisp and a stutter. "So you see," Uncle Eddie said, "we have in Churchill an endomorph with a pronounced proclivity for somatotonia."

"Which means?"

"That he had the body of a mouse and the temperament of a lion. It was this very conflict in his own nature that drove him to greatness."

That was all I needed.

On campus I went about as Sir Winston. I adopted his waddle walk. I scowled with bulldog defiance. And I spoke with what I thought was Churchillian cadence. It might not have been odd if I had been matriculating at Oxford. But there I was flunking at Del Mar Junior College. When Professor Kelly caught me cheating on a test in biology, he demanded to know what I had to say for myself. I barely got it out. "I have nothing to offer but blood, toil, tears, and sweat," I cried.

Dean St. Clair took it out in blood, after which there came considerable tears and sweat on my part.

Charlie Camp, a tall, easygoing classmate, wrote in my annual: "To a fine little shrimp, but try not to be so salty."

And Uncle Eddie wrote from a circus wagon in Florida: "Being short and sassy isn't enough. You have to be smart, too."

A BRIGHT KITE
AND A
PRAYER FOR MA

★

It's hard to sit down at a typewriter at a time like this, but I knew that it was coming, and soon. Now it looks like it is almost upon us—Mother's death, I mean.

I got word Tuesday that she was rushed from the trailer house in Seguin to the hospital in San Antonio, where they slit her throat and inserted tubes to ease her breathing. We thought the cancer would get her, never even considered pneumonia. My father and sister are with her. They say she comes to now and then and that her condition is serious but stable and that they will call if she worsens. As I write I feel awfully out of touch, what with no phone. Ma Bell, the other mother of us all, cut it off when I was in Seguin over the weekend. The fact that this time it is their screw-up and not mine doesn't make me feel any better. I don't have the heart to raise hell. It seems such a minor bother now. I'll settle the bill come payday and AT&T will be seventy-four dollars richer. Big deal. Thank God for friends with phones.

It was early last week that Ma went bananas. That was Dr. Cohen's word for it and he meant it affectionately. Curiously enough it wasn't the cancer, though the lesions have been in her skull for some time, having spread from her breastbone and up her spine. Mother had forgotten to take her nerve-depressant pills and she got shaky and paranoiac, imagining the worst kind of calamities. She thought the people in the trailer court were fighting and she called the police out twice before everyone realized that it was all in her mind. She thought I was lying dead in my coffin here in Dallas, and she raised a ruckus with the old man because he didn't seem concerned about me. They dosed her up good with sedatives and took her to the Guadalupe Valley Memorial Hospital. After a day and night they called Daddy and told him to come after her, that she was violent and that they couldn't handle her. Dr. Moore, the local physician, suggested we might have to commit her. She was throwing things at the nurses and being contrary as all get-out. Daddy went down there and found her sitting at the edge of her bed, naked and defiant. He cussed out everybody and took her home.

By the time my brother and sister and I arrived she was calm and lucid. She had asked Daddy to give her a sponge bath and she had put on her best gown and some lipstick and rouge. I bent over the bed and kissed her.

"You weren't dead, were you?" she said.

"No, not by a long shot. You were just having a bad dream. You were imagining a lot of bad things that weren't true."

"Does it mean I'm losing my mind?" She looked at me acutely, her dark eyes gauged for the slightest suggestion of deception. We had talked about it before, when we learned the cancer had spread to her skull, and she had gotten us to promise that if her mind went we would take her off the chemo and let her die.

"Mother," I said, "Dr. Cohen and Dr. Moore both agree that it isn't the cancer that's causing you to go out of your head. It is the antidepressant that you got off of that's causing the hallucinations. We've got you back on it, in big doses, and already you're doing better. If you slip back over the next day or so, I'll tell you what's right about your thinking and what's wrong."

She squeezed my hand. "I trust you," she said.

"Hey," I said, lying down beside her, "remember when I was a kid and having those nightmares?"

"Yes."

"And remember how you used to take me to the bathroom and wash my face and tell me that it was all just bad dreams and that everything was all right?"

"Yes."

"Well, turnabout is fair play. It's my time to mother you."

"Daddy says I really put one on at the hospital," she said shyly.

I laughed. "Oh, Ma, you pulled a beaut. They'll remember you for a long time."

She giggled.

Then she grew earnest. "Billy," she said, "I wasn't completely crazy. I thought Daddy had put me in an asylum. I didn't know where I was and I kept calling for you and Bobby and Joyce but no one came. I decided that I was going to get out of there if it killed me." She sighed and wondered aloud if Dr. Moore was mad at her.

"No," I said. "He understands."

Later, when Dr. Moore telephoned, Mother got on the line and apologized. Henry Moore is an overworked and harassed doctor in that little town, but he was sweet and made her laugh.

I left Seguin feeling better about her. Bobby and Joyce and I had stopped by to see Steve Cohen, Mother's specialist in San Antonio, and he said that the spunk that she had shown in the Guadalupe hospital was the very thing that had kept her alive these past three years—six, really, if you count the first mastectomy. And he agreed with Joyce's offer to take Mother home to Woodsboro where Joyce could care for her. It would relieve Joyce from making those two-hour trips back and forth and it would give Daddy some rest, and the doctor thought it would do Mother a world of good. Our only fear was selling it to them.

Ma and Pa had never been apart except for the four years he had worked in the oil fields in Saudi Arabia. Oh, they had had their battles and their grudges, but they had stuck together through forty-eight years and the coming and going of children, grandchildren, and great-grandchildren. We went back to Seguin, and Bobby, ever the salesman and always the stalwart when it came to family affairs, why he sold it to them like a preacher selling salvation. Joyce was all excited. She and her husband, Jimmy, would redo a room for Mother and put in an air-conditioner, and we would all meet in Seguin to drive her down to Woodsboro. If she couldn't sit up all the way, we would lay her down in the back of Bobby's station wagon. That would have been today. Damn.

But maybe she'll surprise us and pull through again. She's done it before. Lord knows she's as tenacious as a leech. If she could read this I'm sure she would rally. And so I write and send it up like a bright kite soaring and tugging on a taut string, and wish Mother could look out her window and see it and recover and share with us one more lovely spring.

DEEP WITHIN HER
HEART LIES A MEMORY

★

Aunt Earline writes from Evening Shade, Arkansas, that one of her boarders sat down on her most prized Bob Wills record, the one he made with Merle Haggard just before Wills died, and busted the bejesus out of it. The poor woman is disconsolate, encloses ten bucks and a plea for me to please go out and find her another copy of *For the Last Time*, and mail it to her posthaste.

Well, I'm happy to say that the album is already on its way to the Ozarks. I've been to Evening Shade. I know how boring it can get, even if you're a good-looking old gal running a boardinghouse full of drifters. Once in a while, Earline gets a wild hair and hauls off and drives over to Bald Knob or Thayer, the two nearest towns, but mostly she sits on a bar stool in her kitchen polishing her fingernails and drinking beer and smoking cigarettes and playing country music on the radio or the record player, maybe jawing with one of her good-ol'-boy roomers, while waiting for the ever-present whole haunch-of-a-steer roast in the oven to cook. No matter how big and bawling a hunk of meat she serves up for supper, it is reduced to a bone or two by the time the men leave the long table. Such carnivorous appetites you have never seen. Earline says they'd eat the hooves and tail if she put such as that in front of them.

If you're ever passing through that part of the country, drop in and see old Earline. She'll give you a meal you won't forget, and a room for the night you'd just as soon forget. As a hostess she doesn't put a lot of effort into the amenities. If a pipe breaks, she wraps it in gaff tape. If a roach or a rat runs across the floor, she'll take aim and try to spear it with a high-heeled shoe. But there's always cold beer and Bob Wills. She plays his old records day and night without letup, at such volume you can hear it in an upstairs bedroom with your ears stuffed with cotton wadding and a pillow over your head. And if you look like you can do the Texas Two-Step or Betty's Waltz, she'll come down off of that stool and dance you ragged.

I feel kind of sorry for her. None of the clods she drags around the floor nowadays are anywhere near up to Uncle John. When I see her locked into some galoot's arms, her head on his chest and her eyes rolled back in her head like some blissful cow, I know she's really gone back to Rob's Place in Robstown, Texas. Bob Wills and the Texas Play-boys are swinging up on the bandstand, and Uncle John, tall, sweet-talking, smooth-dancing Uncle John, is pulling her around and around making her dizzy in a way that liquor can never do.

It's funny. The last time I saw the three of them in their prime—I mean Earline and John and Bob Wills—was at a country dance in Yorktown, Texas. It must have been the summer of 1949. Uncle John was working derricks on a big steam rig, and he got me on as a morning-tour roughneck for the summer. Yorktown was German Bohemian country. Every other establishment on the square was a beer hall, and on Saturday nights everyone came from miles to dance at a big pavilion on the edge of town. On this particular Saturday, John and I had to report to the rig before midnight, but we got Earline and went stomping anyhow, because Bob Wills and the Playboys were playing.

We had seen Wills in the movies, had heard him and the old Light Crust Doughboys on the radio, and we had seen him at many a dance, so he was as familiar to us as any famous star, only much more comfortable and neighborly. Hell, he was just an old country boy, too, born and raised in Turkey, Texas, over in Limestone County. He always wore a little belly over his sagging belt, a cigar in the corner of his mouth, and that ten-gallon white hat. And, of course, he carried his fiddle. He never looked flashy, never wore any of that stupid spangle, looked like he had put on starched dress khakis to walk down to the town square and pass the time of day. The only thing expensive about him was that cowboy hat, which must have cost a hundred, and maybe his boots.

When he walked up to the microphone to start the dance, he always said the same thing:

"Howdy, everybody from near and far. You want to know just who we are? We're the Texas Playboys from the Lone Star...."

The fiddles would start to sing and the music would not let up, would not let you rest. You couldn't not dance. If there weren't enough men to go around, women danced with women. I remember that during the break that night, Bob Wills stepped down into the crowd to have a beer, and Earline went up to him and gave him a big kiss. He hugged her, called her "Little Lady," and shook hands with John and me and asked us what we'd like to hear in the next set.

He'd already played "San Antonio Rose" and all those

lyrical tunes that Tommy Duncan and Leon McAuliffe sang so well. So Earline asked him to play the rags, "Texas Playboy," "Lone Star," "Wills Breakdown."

Well, when the band returned, they broke into it, and Earline and John pumped and jigged around that huge hall for all they were worth. They danced everybody off the floor but a couple of diehards, and when it was over they got a big hand, and Bob Wills tipped his hat to them.

John and I had to go to work, but Earline didn't want to leave, so John just said, "Shoot, honey, stay and enjoy yourself. Somebody's bound to take you home." Now that was an understatement. Earline was so good-looking you couldn't stand it. John shouldn't have encouraged her. Maybe she would've done the same thing anyway—in fact I'm sure she would've. You know what I mean. I don't need to go into the details, except to say it was the last time we would see Earline for a while. Finally she came dragging in and John took her back. He was no paragon of virtue himself. He'd done the same thing more than a time or two.

As the years passed, things fell apart.

John ended up in prison and he died there.

Earline went back to Evening Shade.

Bob Wills got old and sick, and after a stroke was confined to a wheelchair. A few years ago, just before his death in the spring of 1975, J. B. Walling threw a tribute for Wills one Monday night in Fort Worth at the Tarrant County Convention Center. It was a big to-do, and Earline came down and we went to see it. It was wonderful, in a way, seeing the old Playboys and all the stars of country music. Roy Acuff, Tex Ritter, Merle Haggard, and many others were there. The actor Chill Wills came, and so did the governor Preston Smith.

But when Bob Wills was rolled out in his wheelchair, when he tried to talk and sing "Take It, Leon," when he tried to yodel the way he used to, it just didn't work. He was practically a dead man. It was pathetic, and Earline cried. "Take me home, Billy," she sniffled. "I can't bear to watch anymore. Bless his poor heart."

MA'S VALIANT BATTLE

★

As the ambulance came to pick her up Monday a week ago, Mother scribbled a note and left it for Daddy to find. She wrote eight words: "I'll have a new home in heaven someday."

By Friday I was convinced her fatalism was prophetic. For four days she had fought for each breath, her cancer-ravaged body rising and falling in a paroxysm of pain and fever as the pneumonia roared like hot lava in her lungs. For three nights my sister Joyce hung by her side in Room 254 at San Antonio's Northeast Baptist Hospital. Then, Thursday night, it was my turn. I gained, in those dark hours, a new respect for Joyce. What you do, instinctively, is breathe each breath with Mother, as if to help, and of course it is emotionally and physically exhausting. Joyce had done it for three nights running, being spelled during the day by our father. Now, after only a single night, I was ready for my brother, Bobby, to relieve me.

It had been a strange, eerie vigil for me as Mother drifted back and forth between the conscious and subconscious world. One minute she would be talking about how her sheepskin kept her from getting bed sores, and the next minute she would be back in the trailer house at Seguin, reminding me in an impatient voice to flush the commode so the cat could drink from it. She would lament that her medicine was costing Daddy one hundred dollars a month, and then she would talk with the dead—her mother and father, Mama and Daddy Harrell—though much of it was dreamy. The words came out as if from a cadaver that had been wound back up and given breath by an insistent respirator. Sometimes her words would run away from her and explode through her lips in bursts of air and spittle. Other times they would come out as if carved at great sacrifice from the scripture of her soul.

"Dr. Cohen gave me six months to live years ago," she managed to say at one point. After that she got weaker and wobbled off into incoherence. Just about the time I thought her mind would never come back, she beckoned me close. She raised a long, shaky talon and presented it to me. "How do my nails look?"

"They look beautiful," I said. "They are a pretty orange."

"I do my nails myself," she said.

Sunrise brought a brutal Friday. Mother's fever went up, her breathing became even more labored, and her blood pressure dropped.

"I've got to see the little boy dance," she gasped, looking at me madly. She sank into a semicoma.

I retreated to the waiting room, worn out with hearing her lungs heave and watching her body rise up and off the bed and quiver and fall. Daddy was due in from Seguin and he was late.

We worry about his driving. He thinks he's a cavalier at the wheel, but he's nearing eighty and handles a car in just about the way you would think.

At last he shows up, stepping stiffly from a wrecker which is towing his bashed-up car. I run out front.

"What's happened?"

"I had a little wreck," he says, waving the wrecker on.

The little wreck involved four vehicles. Miraculously he is only shaken, though his car is out of commission. And he didn't get a ticket. It wasn't his fault. I still can't believe it.

Pa and I sit in the room with Mother. She looks like hell. So does he. He is gray and gaunt and sits there forlornly, his horny old hands anchored like weights in his lap. He has a cut on his elbow, a bruised shoulder, a wrecked car, and a dying wife and he forgot to bring his high blood pressure pills. Suddenly he belches.

"You ate a bunch of cabbage."

It comes from Mother, this teasing quip, and I can't believe it. She is supposed to be out, zonkers, but behind all that fever and fog, down below the cancer and pneumonia, cutting through the drugs and coming up for air, is her old wit.

"Naw, woman," he says. "Sausage."

By the time I head for the airport to pick up Bobby, I have geared myself up again to accept her death. "I need a rest," she has said. "I am tired of breathing. It is such an effort."

"If you stop," I told her, "you're done for."

"I know," she said, "but I don't care. I'm so tired."

I looked at her and felt a great pity. The suffering had left a mark on her that I think will never go away. For the first time, I wished she would stop breathing and die.

Bobby is with her through the night Friday and she is semicomatose and critical. Joyce and her husband, Jimmy, rest in a nearby motel. We have alerted other family members and have made tentative funeral arrangements.

Mother hangs on through Saturday, though by now she is considered comatose. All her life signs are at the lowest ebb. Bobby insists on staying with her. When I go to relieve him just before midnight, I find him trying to talk with her. He is convinced she can hear him, that the moan in her breathing, the darting of an eyebrow, is a signal, her own faint Morse code. I think he is crazy from exhaustion. So do the nurses. We humor him and send him to bed.

I sit and listen to Mother inhale and exhale and I grieve. I look at her and I get angry. She is not alive. Janavee Elizabeth Harrell Porterfield is kaput. The only reason her heart beats and her lungs function is because of the oxygen and the fluids they pump into her.

It is 1:00 A.M. Sunday and Dr. Steve Cohen is home asleep, but I telephone anyway. In essence, what I ask him is, Why continue the masquerade?

"We are doing nothing fancy," he assures me. "But we must maintain the oxygen and fluids until I am convinced the damage that has been done is irreparable. It's not likely, but she could, by some miracle, come back. But don't take heart in that. I'm speaking technically. Certainly she is most grave."

I give up and go to the rooms to sleep. Late Sunday morning Bobby calls from the hospital. "Billy, come on over and speak to your mother."

"Bobby, you wouldn't joke about a thing like this?"

"Come quickly."

Before I enter the room, he hands me the nurses' chart. It says: "10:00 A.M. Sunday. Intermittent responsiveness to verbal stimuli—uttered 'good morning' to nurse and aware of Dr. Cohen's presence."

We go in and Bobby touches her arm.

"Mother, look who's here. It's Billy."

She cocks an eye open and penetrates to the heart of me.

"Mother," Bobby urges, "Billy doesn't believe it. Show us a grin."

She does it. Yes, yes, yes, yes.

★

HOMETOWN

NEIGHBORS AND

RURAL FOLK

★

Sometimes a neighbor whom we have disliked a life-time for his arrogance and conceit lets fall a single, com-monplace remark that shows us another side, another man, really; a man uncertain, and puzzled, and in the dark like ourselves.

— Willa Cather,
Shadows on the Rock

THE WAKEFIELD HOUSE

★

It was the last spring before my fortieth year, and hounded by the specter of middle age and an ever-insistent mediocrity, I had been driving about the countryside for weeks, looking for an empty house in which to burrow myself, old recluse that I was, or so I felt.

Not just any place would do. It had to hit me right, to please me from the road as well as from within. I had in mind woody seclusion, a worn and haughty house with lightning rods and a history hidden in its attic. Andrew Wyeth would paint it, Hawthorne count its gables. Ghosts would haunt it and, after me, tourists, come to see where my genius had at last soared like beautiful bats from some Gothic belfry. Forty does that to the best of men. I drove many a mile and walked through a gloomy forest of creaking boards before I came upon the Wakefield House.

It stood like some tall Victorian lady, and the closer I drew the quieter I became, because time and vandals had done terrible things to her.

Yet there was an integrity about the old ruin that redeemed it. Great care and craftsmanship had gone into its construction, and an incidental sag here and an occasional collapse there only made it more magnificent. Certainly I had never lived in so grand a house, and I walked through the double doors with as much care as curiosity.

That was in May. Within a week I had moved in, much to the amazement of the owner. He was a real-estate speculator who'd bought the acreage as an investment, never dreaming that he could rent out the old house itself. Any fool could see that it was in shambles. He ticked off its drawbacks. It could be a firetrap come the hot summer, and if I lasted into the winter I would find it shaky and drafty in the wind and leaky in the rain. It had no power or plumbing. The water in the hand-dug wells was foul and the cistern was brimming with trash. Fine, I had said, I'll take it. And I did, for thirty-five dollars a month. He hated to take my money, the landlord said, but of course he did.

There were nine rooms. I lived in but one, the parlor with the bay windows overlooking the woods and the trailer park in the distance below. I had to put in panes and screens. Every window had been shattered and the upstairs was a roost of birds. I furnished the parlor with an iron cot, a rough table and chairs, and a couple of trunks. I hauled water in Jerry cans, bathed in a tin tub. I kept foodstuff cool in an old icebox, cooked on an outdoor grill. I dug a hole out back and built an outhouse over it.

It was sweet and comfortable, that spring of 1972, as sweet and comfortable as my privy, and I did all these things in my own good time. Mostly I did a lot of sitting and rocking, stroking my collies and sipping and smoking out there on the long porch, letting my soul cure like a leaf of tobacco in all that old wood and resonance. By sundown I was so enriched I would write well into the lamplit night. It felt good, the writing, and later, when I came to it cold, it read well. Better a late bloomer than no bloomer at all, I told myself.

But you can't live alone in an old house and not have it speak to you of past lives it kept. The ghosts seemed to come out of the walls and tug at me gently. Who were the Wakefields? Where had they come from? Where had they gone? Down at Bartonville, a crossroads store and gas station, they told me to go and ask Mrs. Calvert. She'd been around since Genesis.

It turned out she lived on a little farm across the road from me with her bachelor son, Lewis. She said she'd noticed me hanging around the Wakefield House, saw the pale light at night, and wondered what kind of crazy fool I was. Made her nervous. No one had lived there for years.

The heads of the Wakefield House before I came were Father Time and Cousin Neglect, and before them the patriarch of that corner of the county, Henry Frank Wakefield. He had come from Tennessee before the Civil War, became a man of some substance and local renown. He built a gin and grist mill. Odell Thomas came with his general store. The wagon maker, H. M. Roper, set up shop. Families began to gather round, so many that they built a post office and made Frank Wakefield master, and called the corner halfway after his family, Waketon. Mrs. Calvert didn't know what finally happened to Frank Wakefield. She seemed to remember that he had built the house that bore his name in 1885, and that he had hauled the timber that went into it all the way from Louisiana. She fancied he had been a handsome mustachioed man, that he had buried a couple of wives and had daughters, but she wasn't sure. The years had whisked everyone away as well as much of her memory. Waketon itself was only a dream. It was all so long ago and she had been but a girl.

Someone said I should see Widower Page, the old black man who used to tend graves in the old family cemeteries around and about. He might know where the Wakefields were buried. He lived in a shack down a certain country lane.

An aged black man opened the door of the little house.

"Widower Page?"

"No," he replied, "I'm Widower Smith. Widower Page is down the road."

An aged black man answered the knock at the house down the road.

"Widower Page?"

"No," he said, "he's in the last house down the road."

"Are you a widower too?"

"Yes," he said, "I'm Widower Brandenburg."

I found the last house down the road but I never found Widower Page. I stayed in the Wakefield House for 222 days and nights, until that December, and I never found the *finis* to Frank Wakefield, although I came to believe that he did take a third wife, a much younger woman named Alle. I finished my book, but it never found a publisher, which is just as well because now I can see it wasn't any good.

It was six years ago Sunday, and I found myself drawn there for a final look. The house has collapsed in upon itself. And yet the wells Frank Wakefield dug and walled with brick have not fallen in, and the tools he forged I find work well with new wood in them. The bois d'arc pillars he set and seamed the barn around are as deep and abiding as the Biblical legend which gave them their name. Wood of the Ark. Even with winter coming on I could see his vines grow grapes. The fruit trees he set out still bear plums and apples and figs, the garlic patch is pungent. I don't know how long Frank Wakefield lived and where they put him in the ground. But as Wallace Stevens says, surely about Frank, that it was in the earth only that he was at the bottom of things and of himself.

There he could say
Of this I am, this is the patriarch,
This it is that answers when I ask,
This is the mute, the final sculpture
Around which silence lies on silence.
This repose alike in springtime
And, arbored and bronzed, in autumn.

He said, I had this that I could love, . . .

Everything comes to him
From the middle of his field. . .
There he touches his being, there as he is
He is. The thought that he had found all this
Among men, in a woman—she caught his breath—. . .

is beautiful.

Yes. I remember sitting on his long porch, surrounded by golden dogs, knowing it must have been true.

JUNETEENTH WITH
SASSMOUTH

★

We all knew that Deacon Sassmouth Jesse Cree wasn't old enough to have been a slave, but one of the reasons we white kids slipped off and crashed the big Juneteenth doin's down on Dobie Creek was to see Sassmouth in all his black splendor and hear him tell of slavery days.

He was always the star of the festivities, he and his wife Corinna. In fact, they always staged the holiday, and while they were careful to start it out in the afternoon on a high, sober note with appropriate speeches by black leaders and one or two liberal white dignitaries, their natural exuberance would start poking through the straitlaces along about dark, and then the old campgrounds would rock and sway till the wee hours.

For years I thought this annual root and toot to emancipation was exclusive to the blacks in Little Egypt, a kind of commemorative flare they sent up out of their own proud genius. If its origins proved to be as broad as Texas, it was no more a comedown to me than the realization that Sassmouth's stories were larger and older than his own experiences.

5 6

The Crees would print up handbills and distribute them throughout Froggy Bottom. The invitation was irresistible:

Wear you dress above your knees
And strut your stuff with who you please.
Juneteenth Picnic
at
Sassmouth and Corinna Cree's
Dobie Creek Campground
"Where the Living Dance and the Dead Lie."

That last allusion was to the departed members of Deacon Cree's congregation, who did indeed lie buried just a few yards away. Sassmouth was as nervy as his name. He played musical chairs with the furniture of heaven and hell, and everyone loved it.

Sassmouth would clear away the watermelon leftovers and get up on a picnic table. He would take off his black coat, loosen his tie, and hold you in the wonder of his tongue for as long as he wanted.

"Now you talk about hard times. I have had hard times. I started plowing at eight years old. I was barefooted as a duck. And I used to work in the tobacco patch catching worms off leaves. Marster would come behind me, and if he would find a worm I would have to bite off its head. I remember my sister broke old Marster's clock. He tied a rope round her neck and whipped her I don't know how long. There stood my father, and he could do nothing. There stood my mother, and she could do nothing. There stood the children, and we could do nothing. But I seen the clod put on Marse after freedom come. We all knew that the children of Israel was four hundred years under bondage and God looked down and seen their suffering and brought them out, and that he would do the same for us. I am no mathematician, no biologist, neither grammarian. Like the song say,

> White man goes to college,
> Negro to the field,
> White man learn to read an' write,
> Negro learn to steal.

But when it comes to handling the Bible, I knocks down verbs, breaks up prepositions, and jumps over adjectives. I am a God-sent man. All the education I got, it was out in the fields. The blade of my hoe was my pen, and my slate was the ground. Now the law says, 'Black and white shan't mix.' Who made that law? They made it. I made a law with my hoe, that all weeds must die that I hit . . ."

He would pause, for a long time, until it was so quiet you could hear the minnows in Dobie Creek.

"One day I was in the public square when I met my old master. I had not seen him for nearly thirty years. He said to me,

'Jesse, do you remember me lacerating your back?'

'Yes,' I said.

'Have you forgiven me?'

'Yes, Mars,' I said, 'I have forgiven you.'

He held out his hand to me and said, 'Jesse, come to see me and I will treat you nice. I'm sorry for what I did.'

I said, 'That's all right, Marster, I done left the past behind me.'

I had felt the power of God and had tasted his love, and this had killed all the hate in my heart."

Sometimes Sassmouth would tell stories for us kids. My favorite was the one about the snail, which he told in dialect.

" 'What's the slowest thing you ever saw?'

'A snail was crossin' de road for seven years. Jus as he got across, a tree fell and barely missed him 'bout an inch or two. If he had been where he was six months before, it would er kilt him. De snail looked back at de tree and tole de people, 'See, it pay to be fast.' ' "

I need to explain something here. I have a good memory, but not total recall. I couldn't remember the particulars of everything Sassmouth said, since I was a kid the last time I heard him. But I was lucky. Twenty years later, I came across some sermons and songs in Alan Lomax's *Folk Songs of North America* that were dead ringers of Sassmouth's palaver, making it possible for me to fill in the parts I had forgotten. Obviously, these traveler's tales had come down in an oral tradition that touched many a black American, and Sassmouth, inventive as he was, was happy to carry on the tradition. Fortunately for us, collectors like Lomax, J. Mason Brewer, O. S. Egypt, Charles S. Johnson, J. Masuoka, and Paul Radin came along to record that which might have been lost.

But what about Corinna Cree? Well, you'd have to see her to believe her. She couldn't have been a third of Sassmouth's age. She was so good-looking it made you hurt to look at her, even if you were just a little kid and shy at being white. Every year they elected her Juneteenth Queen. Everyone said she wouldn't be Sassmouth's woman past morning, that he couldn't hold her. But they lived together so long she was even old when he died.

And I'm sure, as Sassmouth would have put it, that they'll rejoice at the big Juneteenth in the sky. He always said he was fixed, pre-fixed, bought at the lamb sale, caught up in the election, and bound for glory. Hallelujah!

THE EAST TEXAS ICARUS

★

Granny Carraway said that time would heal the wound, and of course it has. It even amuses me to remember how downcast and bitter we were, how black was our Christmas because we lost a football game. But it was the most important thing in our lives, a kind of Piney Woods version of the Super Bowl. The fact that it was six-man football did not make it seem small-time to us. We did not know we looked quaint and old-fashioned in our uniforms. We thought everyone wore high-top black shoes with cleats that screwed into the soles. We thought it was neat that you could take your leather helmet and fold it and stick it in your back pocket. And the fatter the football was, the better we liked it. We were used to catching greased pigs.

We were the Saints of the Oklahoma Settlement Assembly of God and they were the Soldiers of the Oklahoma Settlement Church of Christ. And every December we met in a rude pasture down behind the cemetery to settle our denominational differences in sporting fashion. The weeds were mowed, the yardlines were marked off with lime, wooden goals were planted, and bleachers from the baseball field were set up on the sidelines. And everyone in the settlement turned out—the 42½ who belonged to the Assembly of God and the 42½ who belonged to the Church of Christ. The half-person in each congregation was the very full and resonant Christian soul everyone called Granny Carraway.

Cassinda Carolina Cude Carraway was ancient, and in such a state of grace and charity that she had risen above the sectarian schism that had split the town. She went to both churches. And on the day of the big game she did what the president of the United States always does when Army meets Navy. She'd sit on our side for a half and root for us, and then she'd cross over and cheer for the other side. We all loved her. She was the only human being in our neck of the woods who could get along with everybody. She even liked Sam Longmeyer. For this alone Granny Carraway ought to be in the *Guinness Book of Records* under some kind of heading that champions patience and understanding.

In a thicket full of eccentric characters, Sam Longmeyer was so odd he stood out like a sore thumb. He sure was sore, all right, having spent most of his life leaping from his windmill and crashing to earth. You see, he had a passion to fly, not as an aviator in a motor-powered plane, but as a bird with wings. It consumed him. He built wings of every imaginable sort. He would climb to the top of his windmill, which was one of the highest around, fasten the wings to his arms and legs, and leap headlong into the air. Never once did he fly. There was not a time that he even so much as floated for a brief distance. He always plummeted to earth and lay there in a grotesque heap, bruised and broken and bleeding. Sometimes it would put him out of commission for weeks.

But when his bones mended and his head cleared, he would be back in his barn, reading up on aerodynamics, wrestling with Archimedes on flotation, pumping himself up with Newton's propulsion, likening himself to Leonardo da Vinci. He made careful sketches of birds and bats and swore that someday, like an East Texas Icarus, he would wing his way, if not to the sun, then certainly across the pasture.

The result of all this was to drive his wife mad and drive his sons from home. Sam had sent one son after another to the top of the windmill, only to see them flap and fall. You could tell a Longmeyer because whatever nose they had been born with was now a flat snout. They were also cross-eyed and a little slow in school. They usually dropped out and left home, limped off to save themselves from their old man's folly.

Bennie Tom was the exception. He stayed home and stood by his father. When Sam got too old and rickety to rise and fall from the windmill, Bennie Tom took his place, dutifully dive-bombing into that hard-packed earth like a kamikaze pilot. Sam's resource, his unending search for the wings of man, was relentless. Yet Bennie Tom seemed indestructible. He seemed to thrive on being a battering ram. Brother Howard put him in our backfield and he ran through tacklers as though they were yielding ewes.

Behind Bennie Tom we beat the Holy Rollers over in Little Egypt. We ran over the Disciples in Cut 'n' Shoot and tied the Pentecostals in Panorama. We lost to the Baptists in Bonanza, but it was because Bennie Tom was side-lined with a crushed cheek—not from football, but from falling from the windmill. And that's when Brother Howard got Granny Carraway to use her influence over Sam Longmeyer to get him to stop using Bennie Tom as a test pilot until after the football season was over. It worked and we resumed our winning ways.

Well, by now you know what happened. The last game of the year. The square-off with our arch, hometown rivals, the hated Christian Soldiers. We got ready to murder them and Bennie Tom turned up with a broken collarbone. Sam had gotten ants in his pants and couldn't wait to try out a new set of wings. So Bennie Tom had obliged him. We played well, but without him we lost by a touchdown.

It was the first great tragedy of my life. The next year I would see Boss, my old dog, chewed up by a wild boar. I would lose Shirley Ann Boenig to James Otis Smith. But that first one hurt.

The elders in our church didn't handle it all that well, either. They kicked Sam Longmeyer off the membership roll and he carried his letter to Brand X across the road. And poor Bennie Tom, loyal as ever, went with him. We were afraid he would give us fits on the football field, but he never amounted to much after that. Those nose dives from the windmill had taken their toll.

IN ARCHER CITY
EVEN MOVIE FAME
IS FLEETING

★

Out in the vast, dusty plains country just below Wichita Falls, there is a county called Archer. About every ten or fifteen miles you'll come across a town out there, but they don't make much of a dent in the bumper of your mind if you're driving through. What hits you most is the cussedness of the country. It is at once friendly and hostile. Friendly in its soils, which send up good grasses and productive oil sands. Hostile in its distances and high winds. The mesquite and post oak have to hold on for dear life to keep from becoming tumbleweeds. It's no place for a bald-headed man with a hairpiece. Obfuscations and sophistications seem out of place, and writers don't belong.

The reason I say that is because novelist Larry McMurtry is from Archer City, and for a while there with every book he seemed to be saying he was the worse for it. Of course he left Texas a long time ago, lives in Washington, D.C., now.

In his early work McMurtry was a romantic in much the same way that the old cowboys were in his first two novels, and he was bitter about the transformation of Texas from the pastoral to the industrial. Of course between the time of the pure ranches and the corrupt cities there was the small-town era, and McMurtry was none too kind with it either. Which brings us to Archer City, by way of Thalia and Anarene. They are all one and the same, sort of.

You see, Archer City is a fact. It is McMurtry's hometown.

Thalia is a figment. It is where all the action took place in McMurtry's third novel, *The Last Picture Show*, which came out in 1966.

And Anarene is Peter Bogdanovich's film version of Thalia. The movie, also called *The Last Picture Show*, came out in 1972 and is still being shown in reruns from time to time. It was on the late show on Channel 8 Tuesday night. After five years the film still holds up as a masterful and authentic evocation of small-town Texas, true to McMurtry's novel, and a harbinger of similar themes that followed from the pen of Texans like playwright Preston Jones.

And what gloomy goings-on. The McMurtry book and the Bogdanovich film are about the 1950s, about kids growing up in a town running down, about a place so boring that sex is the only out if you miss the Continental Trailways bus.

The fact that the fictional Thalia bore a great resemblance to the real Archer City did not cause much of a stir out there when McMurtry's book first surfaced. The local library did not get the book until 1971, five years after the fact of its publication, and after a year only fifteen people had checked it out—fourteen women and one man, a Mr. Seth Duren.

Mr. Duren was a gentleman and a scholar, and he was not

at all offended by the book. His only complaint was that his glasses kept steaming up. "You had to keep cleaning them off or you'd miss a lot," he said.

But don't get the impression that Seth Duren was talking to himself. He was holding forth in the five-and-dime, where the proprietor, Kenneth Aulds, was selling paperback copies of *The Last Picture Show* at a rate of two a day. Aulds, who was the undertaker too, allowed that that was a brisk pace for Archer City. There were only 1,722 people in town, and already 401 of them had bought the book from Aulds.

What had caused this sudden interest in the hometown boy's book?

Why the movie, of course, the movie Bogdanovich made from the book. It had opened two weeks before at the State Theater in Wichita Falls, and since then Archer Citians had worn out the highway driving the twenty-five miles to see it.

They were going to see themselves, both figuratively and literally. McMurtry had used Archer City as the model for his novel, and damned if Bogdanovich hadn't followed suit, shooting the film on location in Archer City. Why, he even used many of the townspeople as actors. So the film had an unmistakable authenticity. Like McMurtry, Bogdanovich had changed the name of the town, but that didn't keep it from hitting home hard.

The skinny-dipping scene at the rich kid's house in Wichita Falls was a sensational example. Not only had it actually taken place, back when McMurtry was a boy, but there it was up there on the screen with some local high-school kids making their screen debut without a stitch on.

The librarian, Wanda Lewis, said she was "mortified with embarrassment" at some of the scenes.

And the Baptist preacher, Rev. Gene Bynum, called for

the townspeople to rise up and have the film taken off the market.

The chance of that seemed unlikely. There were too many people who wanted to see it. One Saturday, for instance, Pat Aulds, the undertaker's wife, drove the members of her quilting bee into Wichita Falls to see for themselves what all the commotion was about. And Mr. Duren was threatening to go a third time if he could get someone to drive him.

Besides, it had been good for business. The movie company had been in Archer City filming for three months, and almost everyone profited from it. John Robinson, the barber and beautician, got to do the stars' hair. C. P. Pryor's domino parlor, where the poolroom scenes were shot, was world-famous now, and so was the old Royal picture show. Why they even paid Floyd Bates's dog to be in one of the scenes. Gave ol' Fuzz a box of Gainesburgers and gave old Floyd three dollars. Wallace Bedford and his wife, Hazel, and a whole lot of townspeople got parts. Even after the film company left they were getting a little tourist trade.

That was all some years ago, long enough for the excitement to blow over and for Archer City to settle back down to being pretty much what it was when Larry McMurtry was growing up there, give or take a few lives and some storefronts. Seth Duren died three years ago at the age of ninety. Kenneth Aulds wasn't all that old but he's dead too, and now Pat and the kids are running the dime store and the funeral parlor. The Reverend Bynum, defeated in his crusade, finding that his brethren were as capable of wit as they were of wrath, left town for parts unknown. Wanda Lewis, the librarian, moved too, so Christine Hammontree took her place. C. P. Pryor closed his domino parlor and checked into a nursing home, where he's in pretty bad

6 8   *Texas Rhapsody*

shape. Floyd Bates and Fuzz are dead. So are the Bedfords. Larry McMurtry's daddy, Jeff, is dead, and Mrs. McMurtry, Hazel, has moved to Wichita Falls. John Robinson must be close to ninety but he's still up and around and styling hair. He only asks a dollar for a shampoo and set.

Once in a while the movie will come back on late-night TV out of Wichita Falls, and one time they showed it at a drive-in in Wichita—Pat Aulds loaded up a car of friends and went to see it again—and those who catch it find it fascinating and at the same time a little sad. It is a bleak portrait when you come down to it, and the locals who had parts in it are dropping like flies.

THE UGLY MEXICAN

★

When the gringos rolled up in their car to cross the river, Armando left his compadres under the mesquite and approached the Americans.

"If you want to cross over, I have two good burros," he said pleasantly. He knew they would accept and they did. In this Armando had several things going for him. There was no bridge; the only way to cross the Rio Grande into the village of Boquillas was to wade it like a wetback. And then too, Armando was the only burro owner who could speak English. His compadres carried their own poor countrymen back and forth; Armando ferried the rich Americans. There were not many tourists, it was true, because this was in the mountains and desert of the Big Bend, but there were enough to make Armando the richest man in the village after the bartender, Armizo Martinez, and the fluorspar miner, Pepe Cardenas. Everywhere he went, the townspeople greeted Armando with respect, for Armando was good for the town.

His burros had brought a resurgence of foreign trade to Boquillas. Their names were Masaton and Canelo and they were treated with almost the same indulgence as Armando. Before Armando had come with his four-legged ferries, the village had dozed for more than sixty years, since the gringo speculators had closed the silver mine in the nearby Del Carmen Mountains. In the old days, the town had hummed with the vitality that adventurers with money and schemes bring to a place. It had painted its buildings as well as its women. But with the passing of the mine and the passing of time, the color had drained out with each rain, had faded with every drought, and the village had become one again with the brown mountains and the brown river. Except for the flagpole in the square, it was no different from the earliest adobe Indian towns.

This was before Armando and the burros. Now Martinez had painted his bar and had bought a dictionary; Señor Del Barrio had stocked his store with curios and plaster busts of John Fitzgerald Kennedy, and the Benito Juarez federal school had been painted bright blue.

The new commerce had even stimulated the children. Now they ran out to the tourists Armando brought in and tried to sell them rocks. Their parents encouraged them. The marvel of it was that the stupid gringos bought the rocks, the fluorspar. It littered the canyon floor like shells on a seashore, anyone's for the bending down, but the gringos did not seem to notice. This was the way it was.

So on this day Armando brought his American guests into the village with a sense of accomplishment. Their subsequent behavior, however, left him confused.

For one thing, it became quickly clear that they did not intend on buying anything but something cold to drink to refresh themselves from the hot ride over. Instead of shopping, they took pictures with their cameras, and they seemed to like the most commonplace subjects: the dingy adobe huts, a goatskin on a clothesline, an old well. Nothing new interested them and their comments baffled him. They said, among themselves, that it was a shame that tourists were now beginning to trickle in. They shook their heads at the children's industry with the rocks, and one even was offended by the painted buildings. From what Armando could understand, the man preferred earth colors, the very landscape, to the blue and pink of the school and cantina. Yet the man drove a little car of bold red. He wants us to be drab, Armando thought, but not himself. But what could you expect from gringos?

At the house of Pancho Valdez, they all crowded in and listened to Pancho play the guitar and sing. Pancho, the old goat, got very bold. He sang a song about a pig squealing, which the gringos loved, but then in the song he would play with the words and make the gringos out to be pigs. Pancho's wife, Guadalupe, laughed uproariously and Armando laughed nervously, until he saw that the stupid gringos did not catch it.

The Americans left Pancho's house without offering him anything but a handshake and compliments about his performance. Pancho sat in the house fuming, and then sent a nephew out to remind them that he was a professional musician and did not play for nothing.

They responded by handing Carlos a five-dollar bill, such excess, and further confused Armando by their apology. They had wanted to pay Pancho, they explained, but were afraid that it would offend him. Armando scratched his head in bewilderment. In this poor village he had never known a man who was offended by a gift of money.

He did not like them much, but they meant bread, and so Armando agreed to meet them the next noon and take them to a ghost town in the mountains. He waited the next day with a horse, and finally realized that they were not coming. He shrugged and rode back to the village. Gringos could not be counted upon, that was the way they were.

COMING OF AGE
IN JUST ANOTHER
LITTLE TOWN

★

We lived a long time in a town when there were but two telephone operators, and Alice Ulrich and Viva Butler knew everyone's business and where to find them if they didn't answer the ring. This was intrusive at times but it was also reassuring. Somebody cared enough to keep up with you.

Every wide spot in the road had a postmaster or a postmistress, and a football team and a water tower to paint the class colors on, and yes, a family rich and a family poor, a loose woman and a town drunk, and of course more gossips than Carter had little liver pills or Dewey had votes. And I declare it was wonderful, even if rival Refugio beat our butts in everything except basketball. And no, we didn't have a traffic light, at least none that I can remember stopping at. And yes, Elsie Fay French would flunk me for ending a sentence with a preposition.

It was Woodsboro, this place, and it was wonderful because we were young and it was our stomping ground. The earth in those days seemed very solid and good and we were not afraid to dance upon it. It had not always been so.

We were the children of the Depression, and Ma and Pa never let us forget it. We were the nephews and nieces of veterans of the Second World War, which was headline-fresh even in our own memory. With all that calamity past, we rejoiced in the hiatus of peace.

There were no battle scars upon our land, and those that were burned into the limbs and hearts of our war heroes were muted in manful stoicism. Everyone who could walk was home, and we relived the war only in VFW posts and the movies. The Saturday after I ran ninety-five yards for a touchdown against Goliad, Daddy painted the dingy dining-room walls with Kem-Tone, the new miracle interior, and we all went down to the Rialto to see Norman Mailer's *The Naked and the Dead*.

I wanted to take Colleen Glenn but I didn't have the nerve to ask. Colleen was a cheerleader. She had shot past me in height, but the real reason I was shy was because she was so pretty. As I write I am looking at her picture in the high-school annual. With her mane of dark, curly hair Colleen was a Black Irish beauty, but I don't think she ever realized it. Nellie Jo Bunch and Jeanne Crowell were just as comely, in their different ways, but they were aloof and dated older guys. Colleen was just Colleen. She did the things for the class everybody else forgot to do. And she was crazy about her mother and daddy. Every afternoon she went home to Clyde and Mabel, who lived a couple of miles southeast of town on the curve of the New Bayside Highway.

We were innocents but we were full of mischief, even before the onslaught of pimples and puberty. Mr. Piehl didn't want us in his old cotton gin beside the railroad track, but we fought rubber-gun wars there anyway. We ignored the POSTED signs and hunted possum in Kasten's woody pasture. We smoked cedar bark and grapevine, filched watermelons from Mr. McCumber's patch. And it was frightful fun turning over outhouses on Halloween, or slipping up to the Masonic Lodge on Thursday nights and stealing glimpses of our Freemasons as they acted out their secret rites.

I remember Travis Naylor and I, walking home from a DeMolay meeting one night, swearing, like Tom Sawyer and Huckleberry Finn, that we would never get silly over girls the way Hugh Othal West had. Later though, when the sap moved in us, we took the girls out to Eddie Yoland's, where we kissed in the mesquite and swam in the river.

It was good salting down hides in the back of Gilbert Boenig's butcher shop. It was good pulling corn in the hot sun for Hugh Thomas and the Rookes. And best of all was being inducted into the volunteer fire department, where every Tuesday night we played dominoes and practiced fire drills and only once in a great while had to fight a fire.

It was just another little town, I guess, no better or worse than any other, a reflection of the times. The whites looked down on the browns and the blacks, the browns did the same to the blacks, and the blacks, well, they worked hard and played hard and endured it all and never heard nothin' 'bout no welfare. The Scotch and the Irish owned the great ranches, the Germans and Bohemians tilled the rich blackland farms, and every manner of man drifted through the oil fields. But you could cross the racial lines in your work and friendships, and I loved the town. It was ours, after all, and everybody had his place.

A. C. Koontz was our doctor, Arno Walzel the deputy sheriff, Harry Cummins the banker, and Gilbert Boenig was the mayor. Bill Kennedy was the weekly-newspaper editor. Elmo Franklin Norris and Alvis Gregorczyk were the barbers, Helen Riskin Hamilton ran the drugstore and picture show, and Gordie Warren kept the hotel. The Carpenters had a big general store, the Tuttles the biggest grocery, and the Goldens a café. Smoky Heath watched over the pool hall. Graves Toland was the undertaker. G. E. Cavender was president of the school board and Juan Yanez was the janitor. And everybody said the Rookes ran the town because they were the richest.

Having the sense to be in awe of the Rookes was just about the extent of my politics. Now that the war and all the excitement was over, I didn't care that Harry Truman had surprised Tom Dewey and the *Chicago Tribune.* I read only the Sunday comics. I guess I knew that HST was still president because we saw him every Saturday in the Movietone News, but politics without war was boring. Jean Rooke and Dorothy Norris were probably the only ones in our class who could say for sure that Buford Jester was governor and Lyndon Johnson the new U.S. Senator, but then they (Jean and Dorothy, not Buford and Lyndon) were our valedictorian and salutatorian.

What was important was that Aubrey Dean Horner and Keith Hottman were taking us to another district championship in basketball, thanks to the genius of Coach Meyer. What was important was that Colleen Glenn had led the girls to victory in the Orange Grove Basketball Tournament. I had a date at Teen Town with Phyllis Minor, who looked like Hedy Lamarr, and Daddy was going to let me take his car. We would dance to "Goodnight Irene," and later on Lover's Lane I would hum into Phyllis's ear, "I'd love to get you on a slow boat to China, all to myself alone . . ."

A CRACKER JACK
SECRET

★

A Cracker Jack has not sweetened my taste buds for years, I guess not since I was a kid on a perpetual treasure hunt, but the other morning on KAAM Radio, newsgal Vicki Robbins read something that made me salivate, not so much for candied corn but rather for the great expectations of youth. Ms. Robbins reported that the Borden Company, as a promotional gimmick, is adding more than the usual line of surprises to its Cracker Jack boxes. One in every thirty-four million boxes will contain a coupon worth ten thousand dollars.

Now it's true that I ran out immediately and bought a box, but I didn't do it to look for a windfall to pay off the IRS. I'm still a kid in many ways, but that's not one of them. I no longer search for the pot at the end of the rainbow, won't even take the bait from those publishers' clearing house come-ons, don't expect that oilman from Houston to dredge up much of value from the sunken Titanic, even if he finds it. Now it's true that I immediately opened the box, but I didn't do it because I was suddenly hungry for Cracker Jacks. I didn't eat a single one. I knew if I opened the box and found the little gift, my boyhood in rural Texas would come flooding back. It worked. As soon as I spotted the little reward in all that syrupy popcorn I thought of my fat old chum, Chester Garrison.

I don't know where Chester is or what became of him, but if the boy is still in the man, if perhaps he's still a pig lover, I'd bank on his becoming the customer to call the Borden Company's hand. He's the only individual who could buy enough Cracker Jacks to find that one-in-thirty-four-million bonus.

Chester was, to my mind, just another fat kid who could run fast. Well, he did have another distinction. He raised the heftiest hogs of any of the kids in the local chapter of the Future Farmers of America. That is, that's all I thought about him until the winter I went to work in Ferris's Grocery on the square. It was as the stock boy and clerk that I learned of Chester's rather unique obsession. He came to me the second day I was on the job and pulled me off in a corner.

"Say, Billy," he said, "I don't know if you've noticed, but I'm keen on Cracker Jacks. I buy more than the usual, like to collect the prizes. Red Remenschneider"—the guy I had replaced—"always clued me in on the delivery day the new orders came in, you know, so I could get down here before they were all bought out. Keep me in mind now. I'll make it worth your while."

I didn't make much of it at the time. "Sure, Chester," I said.

As he left, he swooped up the last remaining Cracker Jacks in the candy counter and asked Mrs. Ferris to charge them to his mother's account.

"That boy," Mrs. Ferris said, shaking her head. "He never leaves any Cracker Jacks for anyone else. He buys them up at every store in town. If he doesn't die of obesity, all his teeth are going to drop out."

I kept my end of the bargain, Chester kept his. He got first call on Cracker Jacks. I got the first red worn-out inner tubes that showed up at the gas station that Chester's daddy ran. If Chester was into Cracker Jacks, I was into rubber-gun warfare, and it was the considered opinion of all the elastic-arm experts that red rubber loads had more zing and range than black rubber. Sometimes it was so powerful a clothespin could barely hold it. With such an arsenal of red ammo, my brother and sister and I won the rubber-gun tournament at Piehl's cotton gin. I was still not that close to Chester, I didn't run with him as a friend, but I assumed, we all assumed, that he was happily stuffing down all those Cracker Jacks, and, of course, collecting and trading prizes. We were right in no respect.

Some say it was Coach Smith, the new mentor of the boys' track team, who discovered the truth about Chester and his Cracker Jacks. He wanted Chester to run the 220 and the 440 as well as the 100-yard dash, and he was concerned about Chester's weight and wind. Some say it was Mrs. Gilcrest, the school nutritionist and cafeteria cook. She, of course, would have been equally concerned about his diet and health. Still others say it was Red Chongo, the ag teacher, his interest perhaps a bit more obscure.

It was probably a combination of all these factors that led to Chester's ultimate embarrassment. Certainly his parents were involved, for the Cracker Jack bills he had charged at the grocery stores must have built up into a point of contention.

Whatever, Chester Garrison stood revealed before the town as being a bit more elusive than the open-faced boy we took him to be.

COLLEEN, COACH,
AND THE CLASS OF 1950

★

The week I had gotten my failing grade in chemistry had been hell. I couldn't graduate from Woodsboro High without passing, but I couldn't blame anyone but myself.

Mr. Moore, the science teacher, had been firm and even stern but he had been fair. I still didn't know red litmus paper from blue. I could hold all of Coach Meyer's football plays in my head but I couldn't remember Mr. Moore's formulas or make any sense of his potions. He was a new teacher, fresh out of college, and obviously rather high-minded in his expectations. If I was a failure, the rest of the class was a disappointment, and after that year he left us, certainly with disillusionment, but perhaps with some sense of release. But I'm getting ahead of myself.

The day I got Mr. Moore's grade I slipped off behind the school and hid in Kasten's woods and wept my heart out. Russia had just developed the atomic bomb and I remember wishing they'd drop it on me. How could I face my classmates, the whole town? Everybody turned out for Baccalaureate and Commencement. I couldn't not graduate. Heck, there were only twenty-four of us in the whole senior class.

It turned out that Chester did not eat Cracker Jacks. In fact he had no taste for them at all. If he was fat, it was glandular, because he didn't care for sweets and junk food. And all his stories about swapping the prizes were just so much malarkey. He had turned everything he got over to Charlton DeLaney, the horn-rimmed whiz kid who collected everything from snuff bottles to Al Jolson records.

What Chester did with the Cracker Jacks was feed them to his prize hogs. That was the secret that had won him blue ribbon after blue ribbon at the fairs. It made a lot of sense, all that syrup and corn with an occasional peanut thrown in. But for some reason the gossips took it as scandalous, like cheating, like priming your racehorse with a shot of speed. Red Chongo barred Cracker Jacks from FFA feeding troughs, and Chester went about under a stigma until the banker took up with another man's wife and gave us something to really talk about.

It would look funny. Besides, everyone had already written good-byes in my yearbook, including Colleen Glenn.

Ah, good sweet Colleen. I had given up on ever having the nerve to court her, but I still liked to look at her and think that we were friends. "Dear Billy," she had scribbled, "Best of Luck in the future." I know. It wasn't the cutest thing she could have written, as a matter of fact it was pretty matter-of-fact. But I treasured it.

Mr. Moore had given me the word on a Friday. The next morning Coach Meyer was at our door before I had time to rush off to Boenig's Grocery and sell three-button snuff to the farm women. "Let's go outside where we can talk alone," he said. We stood out under the pomegranate tree and he said that the man he really felt sorry for was Mr. Moore because they were going to have to go against him and let me graduate, even though academically and technically Moore was right and had no choice but to flunk me. Coach looked away and sighed. He picked up a rock and threw it onto the top of the chicken coop. "Billy," he said, "you ought to have your butt spanked for goofing off. But there's just no sense in your hanging around high school for a fifth year. Now let's go see Reeves and DeViney and Moore, and whatever passes between us you keep to yourself."

We all met in Mr. DeViney's office. Mr. Moore gave me the course textbook and a copy of the final test and told me to go home and get every answer right, even if I had to look up the answers in the book.

The only classmate I ever told was Colleen, because I knew she would understand. Looking back from the perspective of time, I see that the teachers' solution was the wise and human thing to do. I've made similar compromises now and then for my own students. We live in an imperfect world, and we have to make allowances.

The graduation the year before had been a debacle, in some parents' minds, because of how Mr. DeViney had handled it in the grip of a polio scare. The trustees had voted not to assemble for graduation because of the general ban on crowds. But the seniors wanted something to remember it by, so they got together with Mr. DeViney and cooked up a kind of comic-opera commencement on the last day of school. They put on tow sacks and marched down the hall with their diplomas. It was a light, cheerful note in an otherwise frightening spring, and everyone enjoyed it but some old grouches.

Our graduation was traditional and grand, and as I came down the aisle in mortarboard and gown I caught Mr. Moore's eye. He smiled and forgave me.

We went our separate ways, the seniors of 1950.

Nellie Jo Bunch married a Hodge and moved to Refugio. Jeanne Crowell became a Tucker and went to Luling. Barbara Gregorcyk added Phillips to her name and settled in Bloomington. Delta Mae Koch is a Champion in Portland. Margaret McCumber married a fellow named Fione and lives in Houston. Mary Joe Nesloney is a Richards now, way out in Arizona. Dorothy Norris married a preacher named Housmann and they are in Hobbs, New Mexico. Kathaleen Ragle is a Linney and still in Woodsboro. So is Lillie Belle Tuttle, who married a cowpoke named Wright. Jean Rooke goes by Carter now and lives in Austin.

Half of the thirteen boys stayed close to home. Bennie Tom Earp is a shop foreman in Woodsboro and Travis Naylor is a farmer. Glen Pfeil is not far away in Refugio, where he teaches ag in the public schools. Corpus Christi is the nearest city, and it drew Kenneth Gregorczyk (a cousin of Barbara's who insisted on a different spelling of the family name) and Charles Holmes and Manuel Hernandez.

Kenneth runs a night club, Charles is an auditor, and I don't know what Manuel does. Malcolm Cavender runs a well service in Louise, Bobby McDonnel teaches in Conroe. Ray Hall is a rancher in Phoenix, and Don Summerlin's whereabouts are a mystery. Fred Fricks is an insurance man in Houston and David Evans is an attorney in San Antonio.

Fricks and Evans are always the two who ramrod the class reunions, so I figure they've done about as well as anybody and better than most, or they wouldn't be so eager to get us back together every ten years or so. They both bring a little panache. Fred was once a jet pilot and David served a term in the legislature. Old Travis Naylor's not hurting either with all those thousands of acres in production. But he stays quiet, even at the reunions. I stayed away the last time because I'd just been fired and was down and out and couldn't afford a good cigar, much less the lease on a Cadillac to drive to Woodsboro.

I've saved Colleen for last.

She was married briefly to Eddie Rowland, had a son by him. She took her boy, Dennis, and moved back home with her parents out on the New Bayside Highway. The rest of us went off in twenty-three directions. Colleen, almost in relief, went back to the high school and worked as a secretary to Coach Meyer, who had become principal upon Mr. Reeves's elevation to superintendent. And there she stayed. Meyer retired, her mother died, and her son grew up and married, but Colleen continued. She still had her daddy to look after and all those kids at school. In a sense, the best sense, she never grew up. Her whole life was centered at that school she had first entered as a six-year-old. She kept up with the alumni, could tell you who had graduated when, and where they were and what they were doing.

She never ran out of school days.

Until Wednesday before last.

She was killed in a car wreck between Bonnie View and Bayside. I just got word yesterday.

It is ironic that Colleen was the first of us to go. For it was she who kept us in touch in spite of ourselves. It was she who maintained our identity as old mates. It was a faint tie, held together at best by the cobwebs of occasional memory, held together by her in the indifference of our removal, and because of Colleen I write this and remember it all so vividly in a way I can but poorly express on paper.

Like Alice Ulrich and Viva Butler, our own two telephone operators of old, she cared enough to keep up with us, even by long distance. How small-town and old-style.

Part Three

★

MEN AND WOMEN

★

And every century
Spawn divers queens who die with Antony
But live a great while first with Julius.

—James Branch Cabell,
Retractions

CECILIA AND
THE CONFESSIONS OF
A MALE CHAUVINIST

★

At my age, the reward of bachelorhood is not the freedom to go out with whom I please. The greater benefit is the freedom I have to stay at home with myself.

I lock the door and close the blinds. I unplug the telephone. The whole flat is mine and mine alone. There will be no intrusions. People may ring me up, but I don't answer. I appreciate their interest, and at other times gratefully respond and reciprocate because, of course, I have social needs. But some days I need silence and solitude above all else.

When I am this way certain friends ask, "Is something wrong?" I understand why this would occur to them. I have a tendency, when despondent, to withdraw. I guess I got that from Boss, an old dog I ran with when I was a kid. Boss had the courage of a lion and almost the size, but once in a while he met his match.

The South Texas chaparral in those days was full of big cat and wild hog, not to speak of bull and billy goat, and once in a while Boss would hightail it, go off somewhere to lick his wounds. We would search and call, but he wouldn't come out of hiding until he was good and ready. I am not a carbon copy of that old dog. There are times when I hide for the pleasure and not the pain of it; sometimes it's both. It isn't that I'm necessarily writing or even about to write. That is work, and although it is often pleasurable, it is just as often painful. No, what I'm about on these days of solitude is the soul's savor. I open the cupboard of the past, take down the tea leaves of experience, and try to steep from them one last essence of understanding.

I am not, alas, a futurist. The only way I can look ahead is to recycle the past through the present and hope that history does, indeed, repeat itself. On the other hand, there are times when I hope the opposite is true, that history does not repeat itself. You will see why in a moment.

The years I have spent as a professional journalist, writing on deadline about the here and now, have only increased my private inclination to pursue the past and the people who were a part of mine. It is like the grand finale of a Fellini film, when all the dear old faces and figures come swarming back for one last bittersweet reunion.

It was on a Sunday not long ago that I thus enclosed myself, away from present cares, and, like a backward astronaut, like a Wrong-Way Corrigan, climbed into my time machine for a journey into my childhood.

I went back to the summer of 1944, down to the coast to Corpus Christi, where we lived in a little white house on Savage Lane while Daddy worked in the defense plants along the bay. It was the summer that I met Cecilia. She was my first girl friend, my first true love. She was thirteen. I was twelve. It was very sweet, unforgettable.

My brother couldn't see it. He wasn't up to liking girls yet and he made fun of Cecilia. He said she was stuck-up and used big words, which was true—not the stuck-up part but the hundred-dollar words. You had to have a dictionary to understand her. He said she was all skin and bones, which was true. She was skinny. He said she had haunted eyes, as if she had seen a ghost, which in a sense was true, too. Cecilia did have dark circles under her eyes. She did go about with a lot of dread in her.

I never got her whole story straight. She moved into the neighborhood that summer, was gone just after school started in the fall, and it seemed that all the nightmares she went around with, all the fearful things she had expected, did come down on her, did come to pass.

And yet for all her fatality I found her irresistible.

She was like an exotic fawn, with great doe eyes, and when she stood very long in the same place on her long, thin legs, she trembled. Her tight doeskin jumped and rippled as if nerves were shooting through her. I wanted to protect her from the hunters of the world, so I took her under our back porch where it was cool and quiet and where we would play house without intrusion.

We were too young and too naïve to be sexual. But it was sensual. I remember sweet intimacies and delicately tactile sensations, moments of exquisite tenderness as we played out our childish notions of husband and wife. I began to realize our playacting was terribly important to her because she was afraid that she was going to lose her mother and daddy.

"They are very old," she explained. "I was a December child, quite unexpected. My mother and father are sickly, so you can understand why I am so solicitous of them. They could go at any time." Her big, dark eyes would well up, and she would scramble from under the porch and fly home. Reassured, she would return to me. It seemed to help her, to reinforce her parents' reality and vitality, for us to pretend we were them.

The slightest thing could shatter our secret marriage, or

at least disrupt it for the day. Ma had a habit of opening the kitchen door and emptying the mop bucket onto the porch. As there were cracks between the boards, Cecilia and I got drenched. Once in a while Bobby would get a mean streak in him and poke at us with a long stick. If a siren wailed, Cecilia would imagine that it had to do with disaster at home, and she would run home white-faced, her heart in her throat.

"Nothing's going to happen to them," I tried to tell her one day. "Stop making up bad things."

She looked at me severely. "I don't make things up," she said. "I am prescient. I see these things coming. I don't always see them clearly. Often I get false alarms. But the overall message is unmistakable. We, my mother and father and I, we are marked for tragedy."

I would hold her as tight as I could.

Her father died that July of a heart attack. It turned out that he and his wife were alcoholics, retired professors, people of high intellect, but hopeless sops.

Cecilia enrolled in the Savage Lane School, a grade ahead of me, but after a few weeks her mother took her out and they moved back up East somewhere.

Later we heard that Cecilia had drowned in a boating accident. Now her nightmares became mine. Dream after dream she came to me, garlanded like Ophelia, dead and adrift in strange waters. I still see her at times. She calls to me like a mermaid from the other side of the damned. So you see, all my reveries are not an unmitigated joy.

The years ebbed and flowed like the tides, and I grew up, more or less. There would be other Cecilias, not so fey perhaps, not so fated, but I would play house with them too.

Some of it was just pretend, but thrice, oh my God! The futile repetition of it! Thrice it was for real—the ring, the wedding vow, the honeymoon, the settling in—and of course we thought it was forever. I was just as rapt each time out. I didn't learn very well, did I?

But I don't care, I said. You can have your calloused hearts, shriveled against assault. I hurt, I hide, I heal, and come out again in full-hearted search of that woman who evades me. At least that is what I did for years. It was as if every woman I fell in love with—there were six who really mattered over the thirty-six years after Cecilia—would, for one reason or another, turn out to be a phantom like Cecilia. They dematerialized in my embrace. And yet I continued to search. A sea captain once told me that sailors always yearn for what they can't have, something that is just beyond their reach, a woman, a sight of land, a harbor. And that once they have it, briefly, it is not at all what they thought it would be, that it is a mirage, and so they push off and sail on in search again. I was a sailor of the soul. I don't know if it was conscious or not, but all my metaphors of woman were wet, watery ones. Was it the womb, the sea as mother of us all, some memory of a gilled genesis that gave my heart kinship with the deep? Was it the haunting dreams of Cecilia's drowning? Whatever, the mermaid beckoned. In July of 1955, when I was a young reporter in Houston, I wrote this to a friend:

Dear Rum,

Houston is hot. The temperature's been hovering in the 90s all week. As I work nights on the police beat, I have plenty of time in the day for swims.

Yesterday I went to the Shamrock-Hilton pool. I lay in the sun and watched women lie in the sun, strange and blonde and rich. If I should ever cross the barrier I wonder if they would remain strange and blonde and rich. She'd probably be tiresome, tinted, and a bitch.

The day before I lay on the beaches of Galveston and watched the fat wives in the sun, common and gray and poor. If I should penetrate this barrier I would find them, I think, still common and gray and poor, and a bore.

In my unromantic mood I wandered far off down the beach, far off down the beach from the bitches. I came upon a mermaid on a moss with bright little balloons for breasts, all pink and pointed and perfumed, her hair was tossed. She gazed at me and we swam out to sea, and I think I drowned—for I've looked for myself and can't be found.

If you ever get to sea and happen on a mermaid on a moss, with bright little balloons for breasts, all pink and pointed and perfumed, hair tossed, ask if she has seen Billy.

Well, you can see what I was doing. I did not know until years later the mythological implications of mermaids, that they were sirens, beautiful sea nymphs who sang so enchantingly that they lured sailors to their deaths. Jason and the Argonauts were saved from them by the music of Orpheus, whose songs were lovelier, if you can believe that. Odysseus escaped them by having himself tied to a mast and by stopping the ears of his men.

What I was doing with woman was, in its way, as terrible a thing as my more conventionally chauvinistic male friends were doing with her. They put their women in a pumpkin shell and there they kept them very well—or so they thought. But I put mine on a rock in the sea, the rock both pedestal and gutter. And out there, in the ocean of my imagination, I gave my dream woman a split personality. She was at one and the same time an angel and paragon of virtue (enter the wife and mother) and a bewitcher, a femme fatale (enter the wanton, the castrating woman).

It never occurred to me, until quite recently, that a woman could be just a plain Jane, just as I am just plain Bill. It never struck me that a plain-Jane woman could go through the same flamboyant personality changes and roles that I had. When I found out that even virtuous woman was not all virtue, that even a woman who loved you could look you in the eye and deceive you at the same time, why, what I did in retaliation was to run off and try to stick as many of them as I could with my shillelagh. There, take that! See what a man I am. Oh, what a silly boy! What a silly old menopausal fool! What a self-deceiver! I could love a woman and still deceive her, but that did not make me a Casanova. Down deep inside I was still a true heart. That other stuff wasn't important. Wherever a man's libido led him, the rest did not necessarily follow. This was something a woman could not understand, should not undertake because she would not be able to handle it, would not be able to separate her heart from her desires. Now I know that it was I, the man, who could not handle such a thing in her because it was a threat to me. Now I know that some women can handle it and some can't, just as some men can handle it and some can't.

Now I know that the woman of my dreams had nothing to do with real women. Now I know that the genesis of the very names, Man and Woman, is, in itself, rooted in male ego and chauvinism. The seventies made me aware of this and more. It was truly the decade of the emerging woman, and it continues in individual lives as well as in mass and movements, even in the laboratory.

It is a brave new world, and try as I may, I still panic at times, still look about for the old absolutes of gender.

Remember some time ago when it was announced that they think they've found a way to make babies in women without the male seed?

The more I read of Ruth Daniloff's story in the *Washington Post*, the more I became convinced that it was at least theoretically possible, and, knowing some man-haters the way I do, bound to be put to the acid, ovum test, so to speak.

I could see every other Amazon lesbian in America lining up outside Dr. Pierre Soupart's laboratory at Vanderbilt, their uteruses all atwitter, triumph written across their faces, ready to be fertilized with an artificial sperm—milked not from miserable man but from some vapid virus.

I am not overstating the delight that this would give some women who have given up on bearing children because they have given up on men. As Lucia Valeska of the National Gay Task Force put it to reporter Daniloff, "It's the answer to a number of women's dreams. . . . It's very understandable that women who want to raise children together should want the children to be part of their biological makeup. The question which will be raised is: 'Is this natural?' Which sort of amuses me, because 'naturally' we can do this."

There was, in the story, one final and devastating blow to the male id and ego. Not only do the experiments make the male unnecessary for reproduction, they portend the possibility of his extinction. For only females would issue from such contrivance.

It would be the ultimate castration, the genocide of the male gender.

What a science-fiction nightmare! It sounded so fantastic, in a sick, futuristic way, so cold and contrary to the natural procreation of earthly life. Surely none but the most demented females would consider such conception. No matter how clinical, it was perverse and obscene, an evil aberration and an affront to God. On I went in my alarm. It seemed to me that since time immemorial, the biological triangle of man, woman, and child had been the given, the nuclear unit of human life. To tinker with that was sacrilege, as devastating, genetically and spiritually, as breaking the old taboo against incest. A curse would be laid upon the transgressors. Look at the pathetic mother mouse in Dr. Soupart's lab. Was it silly to suppose she had sensed something was terribly wrong? She had eaten the heads off her babies—twenty of them—as soon as they were born. A woman who bore such a child would send twisted tendencies tailing off into the generations like time bombs, and ever after, her progeny would be among the wounded, victims of genetic shrapnel. There was, I reasoned, no precedent for it in nature.

But then I remembered. God, did I remember.

Biology was rife with androgynous creatures. Edwin Way Teale has calculated that a solitary aphid, the green blight you see on leaves, breeding alone without a partner for but a year, could produce enough mites to reach into space 2,500 light-years.

The Bible had intimations of androgyny.

I remembered that Eve was not born of a mother, that before she was torn from Adam's rib, Adam was both male and female.

I remembered that Jesus was not born of a man's seed.

And I remembered that back before the time of the patriarchs, back before the masculine habit of Judaeo-Christian tradition, some primitive people had it that the world was a matriarchy ruled by goddesses. Mythology was haunted by Mother Earths who were as masculinely fearsome as they were femininely nourishing. China had T'ai Yuan, the great, original holy woman who combined the yin and the yang. India had Annapurna with child at breast, Egypt had Isis, Babylonia Ishtar, all nursing mama monoliths. The Hindu had Kali, the black cannibal queen, and the Aztecs in Mexico had Coatlicue, the mother of life and death who bred herself by devouring human carcasses. The earth is at first without women. Sir Monitor Lizard goes forth and captures another male, cuts away his pride, and takes him as a wife, thus setting the stage for woman.

The battle of the sexes went on, wrestling within one body, then cleaving apart. In the *Symposium* Plato tells the story of the circular beings who lived before people were split into the opposite halves of man and woman. Originally there were three wholes: all male, all female, and male and female. Thus it is that having been separated, we search for our opposite halves of whatever was our original pair. It thus accounts for homosexuality as well as heterosexuality.

In his epic study *The Masks of God*, Joseph Campbell traces the shifts back and forth from matriarchy to patriarchy. He roughs out the development of the human psyche into three chronological steps: The world born of a goddess seeded by a consort; the world born of a goddess seeded by a male warrior-god (the male is growing in power); and the world born of a single male god. It seems obvious that the male, with some giving of ground (allowing the female to carry the child), has maintained, up until now, his relatively new-won dominance over the female.

Now, Dr. Soupart, in his innocent tampering with the mysteries of sex, could tip the scales back in favor of woman. The doctor hasn't come up with something new after all, but something as old as mythological memory. Life in its myriad forms, both monstrous and beatific, insists upon being, regardless of the expression. So Dr. Soupart's fiddling is, in a bizarre way, encouraging.

But as a man, it makes me nervous. I need woman. I need her because I am male, with desires both rutty and tender, but I also need her because I am in some ways female, in vestigial ways that are apparent, in intuitive ways that are more subtle, and I seek in her my submerged, severed self, the twin sister of my brother. I don't want to go it alone into that leveling laboratory, for surely if the Dr. Souparts can make women universes entire unto themselves, they can do the same with men. I don't want that for myself. I want to share the miracle of procreation with woman. It seems to me that the ultimate in human wisdom argues participation, not separation and war between the two sexes.

But if it comes down to splitting the infinitive of *to love*, and the women kick us from their beds and make among themselves only female babies, then I will, with every man who's worth his vinegar, do battle with the whole wretched lot. The Amazons of Asia Minor were celebrated warriors and man-killers, but at Troy they were no match for the likes of Theseus and Achilles. And I'm confident that when we Herculeans go against them we will not be without women. There are bound to be some who cannot resist that old familiar tug when a man comes around. With them we will begin anew the race of men and women.

Back when I was writing about Arbie, I mentioned Rainer Maria Rilke, and quoted his letter prophesying the liberation of women. Here I'd like to use Rilke and his letter more fully.

In the letter, Rilke predicts what has come to pass between modern men and women of the Western world. But before I read a portion of that letter, let me give a little background on the man who wrote it. The scion of an aristocratic but impoverished family of the old Hapsburg monarchy, Rilke was delicate and sickly as a child, but highly sensitive and imaginative, and—much to the dismay of his old soldier father—showed an early bent for poetry and a *decided distaste* for ponies and military school. He married young, begat a daughter, and then secluded himself for most of the rest of his life in order to give himself to poetry. He had friends, of course, but most of the time Rilke was so intent on solitude that he would not even take in a dog as a companion. His wife and daughter lived elsewhere.

Over the years, Rilke wrote a few short stories, hundreds of letters, and thousands of poems. He wrote poems as often as some people make love. The phenomenon of all this prodigious production is that Rilke did not come to his fullest powers, to his masterwork, until the age of forty-seven, which is late for a poet. Most lyric poets are like physicists. They do their best work in their twenties and then self-destruct, die early, and make beautifully romantic legends. Rilke's two masterpieces—*The Sonnets to Orpheus,* which contained twenty-five sonnets, and his *Duino Elegies,* composed of fifty-five sonnets—were written in *twenty days* during the early winter of 1922. He was already failing from a lifelong battle with myeloid leukemia, a rare and painful disease caused by the failure of bone marrow to form red corpuscles in the blood. He did his greatest work in twenty days and then lay down for an extended and agonizing descent into death.

As a man he would have to be described as a good and loving but absentee father and husband. He was a friend, but the solitude—upon which he based his art—was the fuel that fed his genius.

Being a genius, he was at his best when he was intuitive. Whenever Rilke tried to analyze and intellectualize what he and his poetry were about, he ended up with a sterile and pessimistic philosophy. Being profoundly idealistic, he, of all great men, was the most ignorant of politics and the most optimistic in regard to human nature.

But about women he was always intuitive and right, and D. H. Lawrence must have envied him. Which brings us to the prophetic letter Rilke wrote in 1904. He addressed it to a young cadet, Franz Kappus, who had sent him some poetry to criticize. After gently putting down Kappus's banal verse, Rilke launched into an essay on love.

His point was that loving was difficult, too difficult for the young. One had to weather and resonate in order to love, to do the work for which all other work is but preparation. I like Rilke saying this, because he was only twenty-nine at the time. And writing to a kid who was only a few years younger. But to his credit, Rilke applied the necessity of apprenticeship—in the work of poetry as well as in the work of loving—to himself.

To women, Rilke gave all due, especially in the work and art of love. And this is what he prophesied in his letter to the cadet three quarters of a century ago.

The girl and the woman, in their new, their own unfolding, will but in passing be imitators of masculine ways, good and bad, and repeaters of masculine professions. After the uncertainty of such transitions it will become apparent that women were only going through the profusion and the vicissitude of those (often ridiculous) disguises in order to cleanse their own most characteristic nature of the distorting influences of the other sex. Women, in whom life lingers and dwells more immediately, more fruitfully and more confidently, must surely have become fundamentally riper people, more human people, than easygoing man, who is not pulled down below the surface of life by the weight of any fruit of his body, and who, presumptuous and hasty, undervalues what he thinks he loves. This humanity of woman, borne its full time in suffering and humiliation, will come to light when she will have stripped off the conventions of mere femininity in the mutations of her outward status, and those men who do not yet feel it approaching today will be surprised and struck by it. Some day (and for this, particularly in the northern countries, reliable signs are already speaking and shining), some day there will be girls and women whose name will no longer signify merely an opposite of the masculine, but something in itself, something that makes one think, not of any complement and limit, but only of life and existence: the feminine human being.

This advance will (at first much against the will of the outstripped men) change the love-experience, which is now full or error, will alter it from the ground up, reshape it into a relation that is meant to be of one human being to another, no longer of man to woman. And this more human love (that will fulfill itself, infinitely considerate and gentle, and kind and clear in binding and releasing) will resemble that which we are preparing with struggle and toil, the love it consists in this, that two solitudes protect and border and salute each other.

PRETTY SQUARE GUYS

★

Sure, there were girls on Cedar Springs flashier and better-dressed, but Ginny was poetic. That's hard to find in a hooker. She had never been a fox, but her hair was blonde and truly her own—something nice and unexpected in this day of dyes and rinses and wigs. She hadn't taken care of it, though. It lay on her head like a damp, dead alley cat.

But the woman beneath it was alive, more or less. She danced and drank double gins and tonic as if she were enjoying a night off. Her tipsy lilt set her apart from the other prostitutes. She had a certain schoolgirl quality about her that was appealing to men who wished, when they were drunk, that they were still back in college. Of course, after four years on the street Ginny wasn't exactly fresh. Her spirit and her skin were a bit pallid and colorless, like a supermarket pork chop that had been on the shelf too long and handled by too many hands. That's why she needed the gin and the heavy rouge.

The rest of them, her sisters in trade, sat on bar stools, sipping coked-down rum, as coldly sober as April 15, calculating as computers, enterprising as shoeshine boys. And there was Ginny, hanging on a good one, wasting a lot of motion on the dance floor. If her man Harry saw her, she would have hell to pay. You shuddered to think how she would feel in the morning when the sin in gin hit her in the head with a judgment clout.

The amen boys under the neon sign (Christ Died for Our Sins) at the rescue mission could say they told her so, but tonight Ginny's ears were tuned to Buck Owens. "I got the hongries fo' yo' love and I'm waitin' in yo' welfare line," Buck sang on the jukebox. It was a Southern hillbilly sound, Nashville-born, and Ginny, who was as Southern and sensitive and ruined as Blanche Dubois, found it pleasing and somehow pertinent, although she was not a do-gooder giving anything away. She was strictly for sale.

The two men who invited her to have a drink at their table talked finer than the truck driver she'd been dancing with, so Ginny turned on the Walter Benton bit. She quoted his poem, "This Is My Beloved":

Because hate is legislated
written into the primer and the testament,
shot into our blood and brain
like vaccine or vitamins
Because our day is of time,
of hours and the clock-hand turns,
closes the circle upon us;
and black timeless night sucks us in like quicksand,
receives us totally —
I need love more than ever now.
I need your love,
I need love more than hope or money, wisdom or drink.

"More than money?" one of them asked, eyebrow arched. She wrinkled her pug nose. "A girl's gotta make a payday."
"How much?"
She told them and a price was agreed upon for the both

of them, not together but one after another. They were pretty square guys.

"Where do we go?"

"My pad. It's close, just around the corner. But let me make a call first."

She went to a phone and called Harry. "Hey, man," she said, "I'm coming over with two straight boys, okay? See ya in a minute."

She led them down a dark street to the apartment house. Harry came out of his rooms to look them over as they came up the stairs. "You gentlemen enjoy yourselves," he said in benediction.

Inside, Ginny said, "Okay, guys, who goes first?"

"Bud, you go ahead," the quiet one said.

"Naw," Bud said, "you go ahead, Dave. I don't mind waiting."

"No," Dave said.

"Hey, come on!" Ginny said, pulling Dave into the bedroom. "We don't have all night. Don't be afraid to get your feet wet!"

She slammed the door behind them.

As it turned out, he had no intention of getting his feet wet.

He was sweet and apologetic, almost boyish. He was just going through all this to please old Bud. They were old college roommates, hadn't seen one another in years, and were out reliving old times. He was happily married and all that and couldn't they just sit and talk for a while until his time was up?

"Sure," Ginny said. She took his money and they talked. When he got up to go, she loosened his tie and rumpled his hair. They giggled. As he closed the door behind him she heard him say to Bud, "God, what a woman!"

Bud was a big, beefy fellow, very sure of himself. He stripped to his shorts and sat on the edge of the bed looking at her. "Baby," he said, "you're beautiful, but you know I can't go through with this. I've got the wife, the kids, the mortgage, the full catastrophe. You understand. I'm just out for a night on the town with Dave. We haven't seen each other for years, and, well, you know. I just didn't want to seem like a party pooper and spoil things for him."

Ginny winked. "It'll be our secret," she said, taking his money.

"Thanks, baby," he said, relieved. "Let's just talk."

"Sure," she said, "I can catch my breath. I tell ya, your friend is something!"

Bud looked at her funny. Then he reared back. "Oh," he said heartily, "that Dave is a man. Oh, I could tell you some stories about our college days. We cut some doozies. I mean we mowed 'em down. Oh, don't get me wrong the way I'm acting tonight. I mean, well, you know what I mean when I say we wrote the book."

"Sure, hon. You guys wrote the book. I could tell that. Say, you two tigers better scat. Time's up and Harry'll be tapping on the door."

They disappeared into the night, slapping one another on the back and talking at the top of their voices.

MANCE AND ELNORA'S
RIVER BOTTOM LOVE

★

Before he died in 1976, Mance Lipscomb, the Navasota River Bottom blues singer, used to come to Dallas and pick and sing at the Rubaiyat, which Allen Damron ran on McKinney Avenue. One afternoon Damron brought Mance out to the house and we sat under the mimosa tree and sipped whiskey and talked, and I asked Mance, "Is your wife still living?"

"Oh, yeah," he said. "I got a wife, weighs about two hundred twenty-five pounds."

That made her about a hundred pounds heavier than Mance.

"What's her name?"

"Elnora."

"How long you been married?"

"Fifty-seven years."

"I'd sure like to meet Elnora."

"Well, do. Come on down to Navasota and see us."

I did.

One morning Elnora and I sat on the porch of their little house at the edge of town and talked while Mance was out back playing with his greyhound hunting dogs. This is what transpired between us:

BILL: How long's Mance been playing the guitar?

ELNORA: I don't know exactly how long he's been playing. But when I first met him, a schoolgirl, he was playing guitar.

B: Where was that?

E: That was over here in Brazos Bottom.

B: How old were you then?

E: I was about thirteen.

B: Did you think his guitar playing was a lot of foolishness at first or did you . . .

E: Well, I didn't know much about music, because in those days, you know, the old people didn't allow children out. Didn't have no music, just go out in the field and play. I didn't know anything about music, whether 'tis good or bad. I just knowed it was music that Mance played.

B: What's it like to be married to Mance Lipscomb?

E: Oh, I think it's the wonderfullest thing in the world, and that's the reason I hurried up and got him before somebody else did. I figured there wasn't nar' another man. And you know, he was really the first boy I ever fell in love with. When I first seed him. Yeah. And me and my ailing mother was at a festival one night and I said to my auntie, "Ooh, Auntie, I like him." She said, "Why don't you go up and say something to him?" I said, "Naw, I don't know nothing about him. I ain't going to say nothing to him." And every time he'd go to play music, I'd go to stand near to him— thought he'd say something to me. And so he told me, "Say, I say, what fast girl is this little girl here? Say, whichever way I go, she is right up under me. I wish she'd find somewhere to go, 'cause I am bothered by her." And so we all went to Sunday School one Sunday and he was going with another girl at the time. And so the girl was sitting there by me, telling me what to tell the man: she didn't know I liked him. So I told Mance what she said. And Mance said, "You better be talking for yourself, not talking for someone else." And I tell you the truth, I growed six more inches. Oh, they could have put me right on the top. Then we started out.

B: Well, tell me a little bit about your life. You had how many children?

E: I never did have but one boy.

B: What's his name?

E: Mance Junior.

B: Well, tell me a little bit about Mance Junior.

E: Well, all I can tell you is that he's fifty-seven years old, and we've never had to pay a fine for him, he never has been locked up, and if he is, I never knowed it. And the only money we ever been out on him was a doctor bill, up until today. And everybody done give him a good name: Mance Junior.

B: How many kids does he have?

E: Well, I tell you, I think he has twenty-three. I always have to count up on them.

B: And how many grandkids does he have?

E: Thirty.

B: You didn't finish telling me what Mance is like to live with.

E: Oh, he's just all right. Just everything goes along lovely. There's only one confusion we'll have, and that's when he'll come in and put something in the living room I don't want in there, and then we'll have a little argument about that. And then it's off and gone, and we don't have no more.

B: And what does he usually leave in there that you don't like?

E: His shoes [*she laughs*]. He'll put his shoes off and leave them in there and I don't want them in there. I tell him,

"Mance, the living room ain't to put shoes in. That's to live in, set in." He say, "Well, I'm sorry. I won't do it no more." And I say, "Until the next time, and you'll do it the next time." And that's the only argument we'll have. Just off and on, like a hydrant.

B: What's his best quality as a man?

E: Seeing after his home. He never forgets his home. I don't care how far he goes or how long he's gone, he never forgets his family. Always did that, even in his young days directly after we been married. He'd go to town, and he wasn't making much, but we was just getting by, and whatever he made why he'd see to his groceries before he'd spend nar' a nickel, so me and the boy could be happy at home.

B: How do you occupy your time, Mrs. Lipscomb, when he's gone?

E: Go turn the fire down, baby, under that okra. I don't know. I used to see to the cows, and hog, and dogs. But I started worrying with the high blood pressure. I don't have that worry now. The grandchildren and grandboys sure help out a lot.

B: It sounds like you have had a really good life.

E: Sure have. Never did have but a penny. And if we had a penny, we never had no divided money. No sir. All went into one. And I just tell you, they can't get no better than my husband. They may get as good as him, but they can't get no better.

Mance told me later the maddest Elnora ever got at him was when he let some white guys with a tape recorder come into their house very late into the wee hours, after Mance had played all night at a club. Mance was worn out, but he sang for them while they recorded, and when they left they handed him a paper sack, saying, "Here's a little souvenir."

Elnora was blue mad at him, said she was sorry she'd married a derned old guitar picker. Mance said she had the look of an eagle. The light was over her head and she was lying across the bed. Mance opened the sack and found fifty dollars in it. Elnora took it, saying, "I tell you what I'm going to do. I'm going to put this in my pocket." Mance protested. "You know what guitar picker done earned that! It ought to belong to him. He played for it." Elnora said, "Yeah, and you are my husband, and I'm going to keep it."

The white guys made a record out of the tape and Mance became famous, but Elnora never let him get too big for his britches.

THE DEAR MEN
IN HER LIFE

★

It was only four months after the death of her husband that Mrs. Bailey, then well into middle age, gave birth to her only child, Ansel. What she had expected to be a joyous occasion, the unwrapping of a precious, posthumous gift from Mr. Bailey, turned out to be a tragic disappointment. The baby was so huge he had to be taken from her by Caesarean section, and once delivered it was quickly apparent that he would be feeble-minded. She took her poor, defective son home to raise as best she could.

The doctors had prepared her for the worst, surmising that Ansel would not progress beyond the idiot stage. But Mrs. Bailey refused to accept that the die was cast, that Ansel would always remain three years old. She prayed to God, not for a miracle, but for the strength and resource she would need to nurture and fortify the boy to his fullest capacity. She quit her job at the dress shop and took up sewing so she could stay at home with Ansel.

As the years passed, it seemed to her that God had answered her prayers. For Ansel grew into a big, strong man, and while he never attained normal intelligence, he surpassed the doctors' expectations. Mrs. Bailey hated the terms and never used them, but she was proud of the fact that Ansel was classified as being on the cusp between imbecility and moronism, meaning he had achieved a mental age of a seven- to eight-year-old.

The important thing was that Ansel was, within the world that his mother had created for him, a socially adaptable and functioning human being. He could read and write on a second-grade level, and his head was full of fanciful stories he had heard or had made up himself. If he had the imagination of a child, he had the discipline and sense of duty of an adult.

He had his own room and he kept it in admirable order. He got up early every day, made his bed, brushed his teeth, and bathed himself. He always saw to his chores. He helped Mrs. Bailey with the dishes, brought in the mail and the paper, ran errands in the neighborhood, mowed the yard. He was a patient and appreciative gardener. Routine was terribly important to him. When that regularity was disturbed, he tended to panic. Mrs. Bailey was careful to keep things on an even scale. There were only a few things that reduced him to blubbering idiocy. He tended to collapse when he got lost, when little boys were cruel and made fun of him. Mrs. Bailey screened the friends he could play with, watched him like a mother hen.

The best thing about Ansel was his capacity to love. He was gentle and generous, so direct in his gaze that it put people off until they got to know him. He had a special affection for animals and birds and insects, but the person he loved most, outside of God and Jesus and Mrs. Bailey, was Tommy, the kid next door.

Well, Tommy was no longer a kid and he no longer lived next door. But he and Ansel had grown up together, and although Tom was busy with his career and his own family, he always came back into the old neighborhood on Sundays after church to sit in the backyard, weather permitting, and eat homemade ice cream with Mrs. Bailey and Ansel. Once in a while, he would bring his own kids, and they would take Ansel out for hamburgers and a movie.

Sometimes, after Tom left, Mrs. Bailey would go to her room and cry and thank God for bringing a Tom into their lives. For it was he that she counted on to care for Ansel after she was gone. Tom had brought it up himself, when she had been ill with pneumonia, and had assured her that he was financially capable, that he had squared it with his wife and that they were agreed that Ansel would· always have a home and would never be sent to an institution. In her will Mrs. Bailey made Tom the executor of her modest estate, Ansel's guardian, and left him her house.

The only thing about it that bothered Mrs. Bailey was Ansel's dependence on her. She wondered if he could survive her death. She hadn't meant to make him a mother's boy. It had happened because of the way he was to begin with. It had happened because she had committed the rest of her days to making him as full and happy as he could be. They had never been apart except for those few days she had spent in the hospital with pneumonia. Ansel had fared well enough, but she was afraid it was only because he had remained at home, among familiar surroundings. Tom and his wife had spelled one another in staying with him.

One day Mrs. Bailey decided that she should begin preparing Ansel for her departure. After all, she was no spring chicken. As a matter of fact she was into her seventies, and feeling it. She decided to treat him first, so they walked over the Expressway and had supper at the Highland Park·Cafeteria. She let Ansel fill his tray with God knows what. On the way back home she began recalling, in a fond way, all the pets they had had, and how, when they had finally died, Ansel had given each one a fine funeral and burial behind the garage. He still knew where every grave was and who it held, and he cried a little as she talked about them.

"Don't think of them as they are now," she said. "Think of them as they were, so wonderful and alive."

And he did. They played "remember when" all the way home.

But that night, just before bedtime prayers, when she tried to substitute the idea of her own death in place of the pets', Ansel went to pieces. He took her at her word, acted as if her demise was imminent, and clung to her like the frightened child he was. He was so overwrought he almost crushed her.

The mother in her wanted to take it back and tell him to forget the specter she had raised, tell him that everything was going to be all right. But the other parent in her persisted. She felt she had to plant the seed so that even if he buried it for now it would sprout in his subconscious and somehow be dealt with. She gave him nightmares.

During the day he was fine.

But at night he would awake and come to her bedside, his great, moon face in eclipse, and beg her not to die.

She was like a she-wolf weaning her cub. She would lick him. "Don't worry," she would say, "I've got a long time to live. Years. Longer than you can count." But then she would nudge him away. "Still, Ansel, everyone must die. I can't live forever. One day God will come and take me. You've got to accept that and look to Tom."

That was some years ago.

Mrs. Bailey will never know if it would have worked, Ansel carrying on without her as a member of Tom's family.

The reason is because she outlived them both.

Tom went first, of a heart attack, just like that. He had driven himself too hard, tried to be son and brother and husband and father and provider to too many people.

And one morning, a year later, she got up to find Ansel dead in his bed. It was a heart attack, too. He was past forty and obese, really had lived longer than the span the doctors had given him.

"It's a terrible irony, isn't it?" she said the other day as she sat on her porch, blinking in the spring sun. She shook her head and smiled. "None of my men held up very well, did they? But I don't care. They were wonderful, each in his own way."

THE ROSE OF SHARON

★

The moment the woman caught my eye I knew she was trouble. I tried to ignore her, to keep my head down and my nose in the typewriter, but she was not about to let me get away. She didn't say anything. She just looked at me. I have never seen such a haunted, hurt face. She trembled. It was the subtlest semaphore, but the message could not have been clearer if she had seared it upon the hide of my conscience with a branding iron. Help! S.O.S.!

I knew I was a goner. But I kicked and screamed to myself anyway. Why did she have to pick me? All I wanted to do was to get my piece written and get out of the office. It was dark out, everyone but the night crew had gone, and already I was beginning to get anxious about the hunk of beef and garlic I had left roasting in the oven. If I didn't get home it would burn. There was a play I wanted to watch on TV, a book I had to read. It was going to be one of those nights to burrow before the fire and forget the freezing rain. At last I pushed my work aside and looked up at her. I wanted to ask how she got past the guard downstairs, but instead I said, with a gentleness that surprised me, "Can I help you?"

"Oh thank you," she said, and settled into a chair. She started to talk but couldn't get it out. Tears welled in her eyes. While she struggled to compose herself I looked her over. She was a tall, slender woman in her mid-thirties, neatly dressed in black, even down to black pumps. She wore no makeup. Her long red hair was pulled back behind her ears to frame what I imagined to be, on sunnier days, a rather pretty face. She clutched a sack of clothes in one hand and a bulging purse in the other. She is literally out on the street, I thought to myself. Else why is her purse packed like a suitcase? Everything imaginable was spilling out of it, things that you carry with you when you are on the run, living hand to mouth. And yet there was an air of quality about her. My impression was confirmed when she began speaking. She was an educated woman—smart but terribly troubled. Her nails were chewed to the quick.

"My landlady has kicked me out of my room," she said. "I don't know where to go. I've got three dollars to my name and a sore foot that hurts so badly I can barely walk. I spent ten dollars on a visit to a podiatrist, but he couldn't give me much relief." She stopped and wiped her nose on a sleeve. "I don't know," she went on, "sometimes my problems come in so heavy upon me I don't feel I can surmount them. This is one of those nights. I feel like giving up."

She had no family or friends here. She had been in town only since June. She worked at a hotel sorting linen, but she didn't want to call her boss because she was afraid he would fire her. She hadn't gone to work that day because of her foot, and her landlady, seeing her idle, summarily evicted her. "You see," she said, "I owe her on the rent."

All she needed, she insisted, was a place for the night.

I called Suicide Prevention. They referred me to Women's Help. They referred me to the Salvation Army. They said they would take her, but that first she had to be interviewed by a counselor, and one wouldn't be on duty until morning. By the way, they wanted to know, what was her name? When I told them they said, "We've had her before."

I looked at her and she shrank.

"I don't want to go there anymore anyway," she said.

I got on the phone again and tried the various gospel missions. It was the same story. They all knew her. Some said flatly that she had worn out her welcome. At last I found one that would take her. I was stunned when she refused. I thanked them and hung up the phone.

"Look," I said, "we're getting down to the bottom of the barrel. Why won't you let me take you over there?"

"Because they have guards with keys, like in a prison," she cried. "I'm afraid if they shut me up I'll never get out!"

"I won't let them do that!" I shouted back.

"I believe you," she said, "and I thank you for that. But I'm still not going there. I'm afraid they'll try to convert me to their faith, which I find terribly punitive. All they know is hellfire and damnation. My Jesus is a gentler soul. He doesn't want me to go into that lion's den like Daniel."

"I don't know what else to do," I said wearily. "I guess I could give you some money so you could get a room and a meal for the night."

"Bless you," she said. "I'll pray for you."

"You'd better pray for yourself," I replied. Then I was sorry I had said that. It made her cry. She was like a little girl.

I gave her thirty dollars and we went downstairs and out to my car to find a motel for her.

On the way she took off her shoes and wiggled her toes.

"'How beautiful are thy feet with shoes, O prince's daughter!'" she whispered in a singsong.

I looked at her. "You know the Song of Solomon?"

"Oh, yes," she said, "'I am the Rose of Sharon. I will rise now, and go about the city in the streets, and in the broad ways I will seek him whom my soul loveth: I sought him, but I found him not.'"

Poor woman. It was the world's oldest and saddest story.

We tried several motels before she found a vacancy.

She promised to call and let me know how she fared, but I knew she wouldn't. She literally limped out of sight. I went home to a cinder in the oven. I tried later to pump some of the counselors who had handled her case in the missions, but their lips were sealed. "Sharon would be horrified if she knew I had divulged anything of a personal nature to you," one of them said. "It is best that you forget her. Really, take my word for it."